Frazzled

Peter Hans Johansen

CreateSpace, San Diego

Contents

Preface

GAP analysis methods endeavor toward developing visionary solutions to complex problems by bifurcating or simplifying the problem into measurable steps. The combined thesis 'Economic Perils of the Middle-Aged American Worker' and 'The Forgotten Graveyard Worker' attempts toward accomplishing solutions toward a complex problem. For instance, the middle-aged worker being 40 to 75 encounters many hiring challenges created by mythical or psychic superstitions, which eventually develop into lifeline challenges. In addition, 'The Forgotten Graveyard Worker' encounters humanistic challenges combined with company disguises. Unfortunately, creating humanistic challenges such as cancer expand into pre-existing conditions and former company denials. Hence, the combined thesis attempts to create awareness to ongoing confrontational humanistic events.

Economic Perils of the Middle-Aged American Worker

Peter Johansen, MBA/HRM

December 15, 2008

Economic Perils of the Middle-Aged American Worker

Individuals encounter various obstacles through his or her lifetime, which brings many challenges, opportunities, and unfortunate economic dilemmas. However, while various challenges yield rewarding opportunities, discriminatory practices occurring in various workplace settings especially towards older workers develop into economic perils or calamities as is and has been continuously occurring in various organizations. In essence economic perils of significant magnitude create unfortunate economic opportunities.

Nonetheless, while economic turmoil continues for older workers, organizations continue delivering economic turmoil, which adds to an existing economic calamity. Furthermore, company social behaviors create genocidal barriers to opportunities for older workers merely assuming short-lived life spans. As stated by Hyde (2008), "Even though word of the slaughter was reaching America, it seemed of little interest to the press and politicians. Lemkin was outraged" (p. 1). In essence social behaviors of an aging society create negative barriers towards opportunities, which develop into unwanted, unconcerned, or genocidal conditions.

While adverse social behaviors are confronted by older workers, organizations develop or assume various myths, disguises, or denials, which contribute towards unfavorable older worker actions. In other words, day-to-day challenges are encountered by older workers using various means available to an organization. In addition since genocidal events were ignored while genocidal events were occurring, then company actions that create adverse conditions appear additionally ignored.

Nonetheless, corporations of various sizes have stakeholders, which seek equitable fairness within a corporation. In addition stakeholders seek company growth through ethical practices and investments, which contributes to a GDP equation. Unfortunately, unethical practices can erode company investments, which contribute to a declining GDP. However, opportunities or goals can be developed, which minimize unethical practices. Furthermore, modifying existing legal systems can prevent adverse discriminatory practices. In essence changes or overhauls are necessary to achieve existing EEOC goals. In addition organizations such as family court services, which contribute towards economic calamities through discriminatory practices and workforce misalignments, require further overhaul thereby improving intended services.

Nevertheless, while economic perils of the older workers continue, changes in demographic populations additionally continue. In other words, prior baby bursts from pre WWII events followed by baby booms after WWII events, with repeated baby bursts from introduced fertility drugs create a baby bang or economic burst resulting from baby boomer aging, a limited younger workforce, and continued discriminatory practices. In essence a baby boom era from 1946 to 1964 produced an increase in baby population followed by a decrease in baby population, which cannot be misrepresented, changed, or modified in population statistics.

Thus, an economic peril of a middle-aged worker faces many obstacles. What this paper and gap analysis describes is how economic perils from various discriminatory practices can be analyzed and translated into opportunities for employment growth, individual respectability, and recognition through various recommended changes and individual commitments. In addition minimizing discriminatory jitter created by various organizational myths can improve economic dilemmas as experienced in today's global marketplace.

Situation Analysis

Issue and Opportunity Identification

Dilemmas, which later can be converted to opportunities, become part of our every day existence. In other words, individuals encounter various problems, which through time and diligence become solved from reoccurrence. Unfortunately, while some issues become solved from reoccurrence, other dilemmas continue without effective resolutions or accountability in sight. In addition such dilemmas become hidden, masked, or disguised from recognition while other calamity events will bury existing dilemmas. Surprisingly, an unresolved dilemma that is currently buried amidst an economic calamity is age discrimination. In other words, and as media events portrait images, "Is John McCain too old for becoming a president?"

In essence age becomes a barrier to opportunity and individual desires, dreams, goals, and capabilities become questioned. In addition an individual who appears old, no matter how much work or effort that has been placed within a company, his or her talents, trust, and organizational fit is not required. In essence portrayed image or skills are no longer required primarily due to visual appearance. As stated by Kennedy (2008), "…loyalty, dependability, flexibility, trust, and putting in long hours (with absolutely no expectation for additional compensation or recognition) were no longer important." Therefore, age barriers are continuously created, which deny opportunities for individual growth and personal challenges.

Thus, as age barriers deny opportunities, obscure walls, myths, or obstacles are created towards opportunity because individuals' age develops unjustified barriers to persons who desire continued personal growth. In other words, aging becomes a problem towards continued opportunity. In addition and as stated by Dempsey (2004), "Stereotyping older people damages us all. First, it can mean we overlook the resources, skills and experiences which older people place at our disposal" (p. 13). Similarly, as African-American, Jews, female employees, or other ethnic groups are stereotyped for their individual characteristics; older workers become stereotyped because of one's individual characteristic. Furthermore, as stated by Phipps (2006), "By limiting recruitment or selection to a narrow ethnic or gender specific profile, an employer might easily miss the best person for the job in question" (p. 521). Nevertheless, regardless of individual characteristics, uniqueness, ethnicity, gender, political affiliation, or exclusive individuality everyone ages.

However, while ageism creates barriers towards opportunities, opportunities can be established towards removing ageism barriers. In other words, barriers to opportunities create challenges. Similarly, as the Berlin wall came down, barrier walls towards opportunities must come down. In essence, the middle-aged worker desires personal growth, opportunity, and not be positioned in an unwanted, unfit, or mythical job position. As further stated by Johnson, Indvik, and Rawlins (2007), "Opportunity lies in using older workers' skills to fill gaps occasioned by the declining birth rate" (p. 15). In essence possibilities exist towards enhanced employment for older workers, which can be used to fill existing workplace gaps in our organizational society.

Nonetheless, while ageism creates barriers towards opportunities, barriers, hindrances, or falsified myths are generated, which develops further barriers towards opportunities. For instance, individual health insurance costs for an older individual can present barriers towards hiring decisions, which creates

employment limitations towards older individuals. Therefore, an assumption that

healthcare or medical costs for an older worker will be greater than for younger

workers becomes formulated. In essence a healthcare cost-to-cost comparison,

which effects hiring decisions, becomes formulated. Furthermore, healthcare

insurance costs for an older worker are greater than a younger worker, which

generates reduced opportunities for employment. In essence presumed older

worker health-care costs create deterrents towards hiring older workers. As stated

by Scott, Berger, and Garen (1995):

> Since older workers are more costly to insure, their labor market opportunities relative to those of younger workers may be substantially reduced. Given these cost differences, it is reasonable to hypothesize that health insurance can be an important consideration in a firm's decision to hire older workers (p. 775).

Thus, while health-care myths develop stereotyping towards older

individuals, who effect hiring decisions, peer review data contradicts health-care

myths towards older individuals. As stated by Johnson, Indvik, and Rawlins

(2007):

> Bureau of Labor Statistics show that in 2002, those age 25-54 made up about 76% of the work population and experienced 75% of the recordable work injuries involving days away from work. Those age 55 and older accounted for approximately 13.6% of the working population and contributed to only 10.4% of the recordable injuries involving days away from work. The productivity data show that those people in the 55+ age

bracket also appear to be more productive than their younger counterparts (p. 15).

However, while health-care myths create barriers towards hiring decisions, opportunities arise that can transform health-care myths into realties. In other words, hiring decisions should be based on individual capabilities such as person-based structures rather than on anticipated health-care costs of an individual. In essence can an individual perform the specific task and does an individual have the necessary skill sets to perform an assignment? Thus, hiring decisions should be based on skill-sets, capabilities, and educational knowledge rather than on health-care costs of an individual. As stated by the Edmonton Journal (1992), "Health care premiums are less because older workers usually have no dependent children and are sick less often" (p. C.9).

Nonetheless, while barriers and myths continue, individual appearances are required and create barriers to employment. For instance, employment training agencies suggest limiting experience years on a resume. In other words, the resume is disguised to show minimal working experiences, thereby disguising individual age. Furthermore, additional disguises through plastic surgery, cosmetic surgery, or hair modifications are required to construct a younger look. In essence the employer seeks a younger person to fulfill the job role, which requires an older worker to make distinguishable changes.

Nevertheless, as stated by Rasche, (2006), ""…does erasing the signs of age on the female face undermine an actress's work and challenge the autonomy of her performance?" (p. 1). Unfortunately, regardless of creativity that is used towards changing appearance for employment, individual ageing processes have not been altered. In other words, having plastic surgery or hair modifications to aid towards employment does not alter an individual's age. As stated by Brosi and Kleiner (1999), "Companies want to promote an image of a young, mobile staff. 'We are a young company of young people'" (p. 100).

However, while appearances create obstacles towards employment, opportunities can be developed, which removes obstacles towards employment. In essence hiring decisions should not be based on individual appearance or years of remaining life rather than on individual capabilities. In essence can an individual perform the specific undertaking and does an individual have necessary skill sets to perform the required task? Thus, hiring decisions should be based on skill-sets, capabilities, and educational knowledge rather than on appearance of an individual or on a remaining life-span. However, as stated by Gerry (2008), "…aging in today's youth-obsessed society, with its negative myths and attitudes about older people, makes the prospect even more dreadful. Being an 'older person' in America is the prune pits" (p. PF.4). In other words, challenges or opportunities lie ahead towards removing negative myths and showing respect towards an aged society.

Nonetheless, while myths and stereotyping continues older worker disrespectfulness towards human capital improvements additionally continue. In other words, individual education and personal experiences appear less valued towards an aged society. Furthermore, employers assume that older workers typically demand higher salaries for their respective experiences. In essence employers disrespect individual education and experience of older workers. Thus, an assumption exists that older workers produce less value than a younger worker similarly, as a female worker produces less value than a male worker or as an African-American worker produces less value than a Caucasian worker. Thus, employers assume older workers should earn less than younger worker, which is similar to female workers, should earn less than male workers.

Therefore, as training myths continue, disrespect towards older workers for training, personal experiences, and hiring practice additionally continues. As stated by Alster (2005), "The suit also contends that younger workers were more likely than their older colleagues to receive training that led to promotions and raises" (p. 3.3). As further stated by Woolnough (2004), "Experience is no longer the most valuable commodity for the HR professional, with the majority of over-50s earning less than their younger counterparts" (p. 1). In essence greater respect is given towards a younger generation through higher salaries yet hiring practice complaints for experienced older workers continue. Thus, as stated by Woolnough (2004), "Industry experts believe employers are more concerned about the recruitment and retention of younger employees, and are therefore prepared to pay them inflated bonuses and higher salary increases" (p. 1). In essence employer messages desire younger workers, which are available for training and prefer training investments towards a younger workforce. Furthermore employers' judgments towards individuals working years or useful life remaining produces further deterrents towards training or company opportunities.

However, while training myths continue, opportunities for training and recognition should become available for all individuals. Similarly, as the African-American was able to move more freely in a slavery society, older workers should be given additional opportunities, which can stimulate their intellectual wisdom and move more freely towards further opportunities. In addition, as Nobel Prize winners receive recognition for their achievements, employers have further opportunities towards recognizing individual achievements.

In essence employers have an opportunity to recognize that human capital improvements consist of personal experiences, training, educational pursuits, sacrifices, and other life experiences. Furthermore, human capital improvements have values that increase similar as individuals pursue higher learning. However, individuals should not be treated as depreciating assets or switches, which can be written off as a worthless commodity that creates continued   disrespect towards an aged society. As stated by Graham (1996), "Contrary to myth, 60-year-old employees have not yet turned into pitiless, prune-juice-drinking, nurse-dependent creatures" (F.1).

Unfortunately, as myths and stereotyping continues, attitude towards older workers or false attitude impressions create further barriers or handicaps toward employment opportunities. In other words, misguided myths create forced early retirement, lack of internal opportunities, or hiring dilemmas, which sends unwanted messages for an aged society. Thus, employers assume older workers have an attitude problem, which creates difficulty in a working environment. Therefore, employers develop unproven myths and create an environment not inductive for an older worker. In essence a working environment created by an organization can change individual behaviors, which causes an organization to blame older workers for his or her behavior. As stated by Martinez and Kleiner (1993), "Most of the discrimination of older workers appears to be based on myths about performance, reliability, and attendance, instead of reality" (p. 1).

While employer attitude problems towards older workers continue, older workers must continuously fight off false myths, which create continued dilemmas for older workers. As stated by Shearring (1992), "It seems bizarre to label people as if they are a commodity stamped with a "sell-by" date…" (p. 11). In other words, older workers continuously struggle towards coexistence in a workplace; however, stigmas such as out-of-date or expired create personal struggles that older workers must cope within themselves.

However, while employer attitudes towards older workers continue, opportunities for attitude refinements create challenges within a workplace. Thus, employers have an opportunity to show respect and stop unwanted myths by creating environments of person-based structures. In other words, treating older workers should be geared towards capabilities and respect of an individual. Furthermore, recognizing employees or older workers within an organization are customers within that organization thereby changing attitudes that develops or influences person-based structures. As stated by Berry and Carbone (2007), "Organizations must think far more deeply about customers' emotional needs and understand how the consistency and effectiveness of clues evoke the emotions that create their customers' experiences of the company" (p. 26).

Nonetheless, as stereotypes continue, additional stereotypes towards older workers create further dilemmas. For instance, older workers receive barriers towards training creating company incapable training myths. For instance, employers assume older workers use outdated methods. In essence employers are

16

biased towards younger workers and assume older workers are not capable of learning new methods nor will be available using new methods. Therefore, older workers are refrained from learning new company skills. As stated by Gibson, Zerbe, and Franken (1993), "The older job hunter is seen as technologically obsolete. More than half of the responses in this category concerned the perception that older job hunter's 'have a poor education', 'lack the appropriate training' and are 'stuck in their trade'" (p. 321).

While older workers face dilemmas towards retraining, older workers additionally face disillusionment in retraining. In other words, why would a company invest resources in an older worker when the older worker might not be present tomorrow? In essence, employer shortsightedness and life remaining obstacles creates barriers towards further opportunities. As stated by Walberg (2007):

> Unfortunately, more than half of the seniors surveyed felt that there is still significant age discrimination in the workplace and about a third felt that the most important barrier keeping older workers from finding jobs is that employers think older people can't learn new skills (p. B.8).

However, as myths towards retraining capabilities continue, opportunities for enhanced training can reignite older workers fortitude. Furthermore, employers have an opportunity to recognize older workers or middle-aged workers have capabilities in learning new skills or trades similar as younger workers can learn new skills. As stated by Paul and Townsend (1993), "Not only do they have the ability but they also have the desire to learn" (p. 67). In essence older workers desire opportunities and have learning capabilities similar to younger workers. As further stated by Walberg (2007), "The fact is, many older people learn differently, but they retain new skills better and they are more reliable and dedicated than younger workers" (p. B.8).

Nevertheless, while stereotyping or discriminatory practices continue, discriminatory practices through clever disguises will additionally continue. In other words, placing chocolate syrup on vanilla ice cream or having plastic surgery for a younger appearance does not change the originality of content. Thus, discrimination with creative disguises is still considered discrimination. As stated by Gover and McClure (2004), "Salary curves typically show corporate engineers' salaries declining after age 45. Companies often go to great lengths to disguise this obvious discriminatory practice" (p. 1).

Furthermore, employers find different methods, loop holes, or disguises towards age discrimination, which create challenges for older workers. In other words, employers will proceed at enormous lengths to hide or disguise any and all discriminatory issues. As stated by Osborne and McCann (2008), "In cases such as Ford, Goodyear, and Capital One, forced ranking was alleged to have been a purposeful disguise for intentional age discrimination" (p. 1). In essence employers will pursue at great lengths using various methods of disguises towards individual classes. As stated by the United States Department of Justice (2008), "Sometimes, housing providers try to disguise their discrimination by giving false information about availability of housing, either saying that nothing was available or steering homeseekers to certain areas based on race" (p. 1).

However, while discriminatory disguises create dilemmas in a workplace, opportunities towards removing disguises should be encouraged. In other words, opportunities exist, which removes loop holes or other discriminatory disguise dilemmas. Similarly, as an African American fought continuously to remove the stigma of racial discrimination or the Jew who fought endlessly over discriminatory events, can older individuals strive for opportunities, which remove disguises of discrimination.

On the other hand, while discriminatory practices continue, other symptoms resulting from discriminatory practices additionally continue, which fuels anxiety and other social dilemmas. In other words, effects of continued discriminatory practices have unwanted health symptoms, which can be preventable if individuals are recognized as human beings. As stated by Marshall (2007), "Perceived discrimination can have consequences in its own right, affecting health, well-being and occupational behavior" (p. 257).

Unfortunately, discriminatory practices continue fueling additional damages towards ordinary older individuals. In other words, discrimination through company reorganization and age hiring dilemmas fuels various forms of social problems such as depression, anxiety, or divorce. In essence age discrimination symptoms as encountered by African Americans, the Jewish population, or other ethnic groups create similar dilemmas for old-age skilled workers. Furthermore discriminatory behaviors towards an older workforce create mental and physical problems similar as encountered by other minority populations. In addition discriminatory symptoms do not become recognized until encountered in discriminatory actions. As stated by Schulz, Gravlee, Williams, Israel, et al (2006), "…everyday encounters with discrimination are causally associated with poor mental and physical health outcomes" (p. 1265).

In essence disrespect towards an older generation fuels unwanted health situations, which can be easily preventable. As stated by Ryan, Szechtman, and Bodkin (1992), "… attitudes towards older people are more negative than those towards younger people and that the differences from evaluations of young adults were greater when competence (as compared to personality) was assessed …" (p. 96). Thus, continued negative attitudes or biases towards an older generation can have consequences leading towards various health conditions. As stated by Grant (1996), "Negative stereotyping in society can lead to viewing elderly people in a deprecatory manner and as less valuable members of society" (p. 9). As further stated by Laskey (2008), "Age-based discrimination can decrease one's self-esteem; it can cause feelings of stress, anxiety, guilt, shame, or helplessness" (p. 1). In essence age discrimination can develop various health problems resulting from adverse conditions encountered in a workplace or other establishments.

However, while health dilemmas exist resulting from age discrimination, opportunities can be developed, which fight to prevent and reduce health dilemmas resulting from age discrimination. Thus, opportunities can be generated, which eliminate age discrimination resulting in improvements towards social and mental health well being. In essence an older worker can be a productive member of society, which can improve his or her personal stigma.
Unfortunately, as stated by Peacock (2007), "…63% of older people feel the government is not doing enough to combat ageism" (p. 1). Thus, challenges lie ahead towards combating unwanted ageism and out-of-date individuals.

Nonetheless, while stereotyping, false myths, and other discriminatory dilemmas continue financial handicaps in resolving discriminatory dilemmas create further barriers towards equitable justice. In other words, individual financial resources limit equitable justice thereby allowing companies to take advantage of individual financial limitations. As stated by Michigan Chronicle (2000), "…surmounting barriers to equal justice that affect millions of low-income individuals and families" (p. B10). In essence equitable justice is limited by individual financial barriers thereby allowing discriminatory practices to continue.

In addition employees find limited recourse towards unwanted hiring, involuntary layoff, or other labor law violations due to limited financial resources. In essence limited money resources prevent discoveries and equitable justice resolutions. Thus, limited money resources causes an individual to 'throw in the towel,' which unfortunately, allows unethical practices to continue. As stated by the Equal Access to Justice Commission (2008), "The report decried the lack of adequate legal representation for people in poverty who found themselves involved in civil litigation in which critical legal matters such as child custody, eviction, employment, and others were being decided by the courts" (p. 1).

However, as legal limitation towards equitable justice continues, opportunities for equitable and reasonable justice should become available for all individuals. In essence establishing methods for equitable justice could create deterrents toward labor law violations. Furthermore, individuals should not be cornered into unwanted decisions such as payments for rent vice legal services for justice. As stated by Brooks (1997), "…the Equal Employment Opportunity Commission (EEOC) and indicated the necessity to have the laws enforced with the agency fully staffed and funded in order to ensure that the EEOC can effectively enforce federal legislation that prohibits discriminatory practices in employment" (p. 10).

Nevertheless, while financial barriers create dilemmas for equitable justice, other organizations such as the Family Court system create barriers or additional dilemmas, which contribute to an existing employment or economic dilemma. In other words, the Family Court system seeks resolution towards employment. Individuals should be employed regardless of his or her prior occupation. Thus, requiring individuals to seek any type of employment creates employment misalignment and bridges to nowhere. In essence individuals establish a Family Court system requirement; however, individuals become entangled in a process, which further creates economic dilemmas. Furthermore, when individuals become unemployed, no restitution becomes available, which further adds to an existing stressful situation. As stated by Orr (2004), "For many people, the family courts have been a problem for years. The power they have is more absolute in some ways than the criminal courts" (p. 21).

In addition Family Court systems create barriers to opportunity by creating individual misalignments that satisfy Family Court requirements rather than individual endeavors. In other words, a Family Court system is not interested in listening to unemployment dilemmas, discriminatory hiring practices, or aligning an individual with respective employment positions rather than meeting current a

Family Court agenda. Unfortunately, misalignment in a workplace develops an unproductive workplace. As stated by Shapiro (2005), "I am often knocked over and thrown off course by tidal waves of absolute power, absolute stupidity, and greed" (p. 196).

Unfortunately, while Family Court barriers exists creating misaligned workers due to Family Court pressures, opportunities are encouraged in a family court system, which will minimize employee alignment through equitable fairness. In other words, individuals should not be burdened with undo pressures from Family Court, economic calamities, and age handicap dilemmas while another party awaits compensation. In addition equitable compensation relief should be encouraged, which further removes undue stresses while individuals seek employment during various economic times.

Stakeholder Perspectives/Ethical Dilemmas

Stakeholder perspectives affecting economic perils are the United States government, United States corporations, and United States shareholders. In essence stakeholder perspectives affect a majority of the United States population. In the meantime, the United States government seeks growth, stability, and economic fairness, which creates gradual increases in the Gross Domestic Product (GDP). However, creating economic fairness requires a workforce that is aligned within their capabilities, which can strengthen an existing workforce. As stated by

Frank, Forbes, Soros, and Brittan et al (2004), "The position has become the single most influential office affecting national economic policy, and Stiglitz's commitment to and understanding of the importance of combining economic growth with a concern for economic fairness are sorely needed" (p. 44). In essence strive towards economic fairness can be a key towards an existing economic crises.

In the mean time, the United States government should focus towards improving GDP variables. GDP as stated by McConnell and Brue (2004), "We can determine GDP as the value of output by summing all expenditures on that output" (p. 115). As otherwise stated by McConnell and Brue (2004), "Consumption expenditures by households, investment expenditures by businesses, government purchases of goods and services, and expenditures by foreigners" (p. 115) defines the GDP equation.

However, ethical dilemmas can arise, which causes a decrease in the GDP equation. For instance, keeping all variables constant except investment expenditures (I) and decreasing profit expenditures from punitive damages can result in decreasing investment expenditures and a decreasing GDP. In addition combining the effects of various discriminatory practices increases punitive damages and decreases investment expenditures, which further erodes the GDP equation. As stated by Lawson (2005), "Discrimination hurts profits, but managers are willing to pay for it, making up for the losses in order to be allowed

to hire fewer workers from groups they dislike" (p. 1).

Nonetheless, United States corporations seek growth through investments

that contribute towards shareholders through increased share values and growth

towards the GDP. However, achieving goals towards GDP and shareholder value

requires equitable fairness and corporate ethics. In essence through ethics and

regulatory compliances can United States corporations achieve gradual growth of

the GDP. As stated by Rogers, Ogbuehi, and Kochunny (1995), "…corporations'

contract with society allows the corporation to maximize profits so long as profit-

making does not cause avoidable harm" (p. 11). Unfortunately, corporations

which exceed profits through excessive greed create continued harm upon society,

which affects the GDP through decreased business investments. As further stated

by Vidal (2006), "…the role of ethics and high standards and how these qualities

drive a business to grow to the next level" (p. 1) should contribute to an ethical

society.

Nevertheless, United States shareholders seek growth in shareholder value.

However, shareholders seek growth through equitable fairness and ethical

behavior. In essence shareholders desire increased shareholder growth through

corporate ethics and regulatory compliance. As stated by Rogers, Ogbuehi, and

Kochunny (1995), "To view their business activities in developing countries primarily as sources of profits provides a less than morally defensible position and sends the wrong signal to developing countries" (p. 11). Therefore, shareholders desire growth through equitable fairness rather than growth through unethical practices or greed. As further stated by Tudway and Pascal (2006), "Whilst profit and stock market appreciation may point to levels of outstanding achievement, this misses out altogether the negative social, economic and environmental externalities that also arrive alongside narrowly based measures of achievement" (p. 305). In other words, promoting child-slave labor or continuously disregarding middle-aged workers while receiving golden parachutes or exceedingly-compensated rewards transmits depressing messages upon shareholders and surrounding society.

End-State Vision

As stated by the University of Phoenix gap analysis program, "A true leader not only works on solving the problem, but also thinks beyond the crisis by implementing measures to prevent the problem from happening again" (p. 1). In essence thorough knowledge and understanding of dilemmas should provide methods for prevention and continuous prevention of existing dilemmas. In other words, existing discriminatory practices towards older individuals regardless of race should be abandoned although various discriminatory practices, disguises, or denials are present causing further discriminatory practices. As stated by O'Boyle

(2001), "Discrimination, unfortunately, exists in forms as myriad as the creative perverseness of human beings can provide" (p. 959). Unfortunately, when age discriminatory practices continue, holistic events similar experienced by a Jewish population will produce massive economic calamities as experienced by a baby-boomer generation. As further stated by Overell (2005), "On the other hand, prejudice is a denial of individuality, and age is no marker of competence. What is jokey in one context can quickly be switched into a nasty tool for demeaning someone in another" (p. 8).

However, as discriminatory practices continue, visions or goals towards stopping discriminatory practices must be developed. In other words, old age discrimination created by disguised company reorganizations and delayed hiring practices through developing an economic individual value system is encouraged. In essence respect towards aged individuality recognizing personal achievements, education, and training has an economic value not related as a depreciating asset. Individual economic values can be developed using a five-year FICA income average based upon highest achieved earnings. In addition current unemployed workers especially individuals over 50 can be easily identified from Employment Development Department (EDD) or other sources. Thus, individuals can and work simultaneous with EDD or American Advancement of Retried Personal (AARP) personal on completing and achieving an individual economic value, which is a first step and will be used towards enhancing individual self respect and stopping adverse discriminatory practices.

As stated by Lander and Reinstein (2005), "The results show that the companies that use economic value alignment increase their value significantly over those that do not" (p. 433). In essence developing individual economic values serves as creating an alignment towards actual individual economic value. Furthermore, individual economic value determines the individual stipend as a result of unwanted employment created by discriminatory behavior. Thus, as fisherman are unable to fish, as farmers are unable to plant, old-age workers are unable to work created by continued hiring discriminatory practices. However, individual stipends become only available when through individual and unsuccessful efforts of finding employment and becoming a victim of involuntary downsizing. In addition adjusted individual stipends become available when current employment is not aligned with individual economic value. In other words, prior engineering professionals working as a customer service representative due to unwanted hiring practices creates economic dilemmas for an engineering professional. Economic expenses, which have occurred in higher responsible positions, develop into economic dilemmas for many individuals. For instance, as stated by CNN Money (2008), "Her part-time position pays $250-$350 a week - a far cry from the $72,000 a year she made as a loan processor…"

(p. 1). Therefore, the loan processor developed an annual economic loss of $53, 800. However, when multiplying continuous individual economic losses across a country-wide spectrum, then economic dilemmas will occur. Thus, valid economic loss conditions are required for receiving individual economic value stipends, which establishes accountability or checks and balances within an economic system.

Accordingly, as individual economic stipends are received by misaligned or disadvantaged older workers, individual economic stipends will develop into an economic stimulus or catalyst towards other economic activity. In other words, individual economic value stipends become subject to federal, state, and social security taxes. Furthermore, the individual economic value stipends allow individuals to continue his or her expenditures. However, while individual economic stipends create a short-term economic stimulus, individual economic value stipends serve as incentives and accountability towards future employment, realignment, and minimized discriminatory practices.

In essence restoring individual equitable value of old age workers through converting economic value stipends into individual economic tax credits develops incentives for future hiring practices. Furthermore, individual economic tax credits become employer tax credits and incentives towards hiring old-age individuals and generate accountability through ethical reporting. In addition similar as bank interest rates are reduced to encourage borrowing, as black Friday events are created to encourage consumer spending, business income taxes should be further reduced to encourage old-age hiring practices. Therefore, combined incentive efforts through individual tax credits and reduced business taxes provide encouragement toward hiring older capable workers and develop employment opportunities, which were reduced in a compressed employment market. As stated by Fay and Thompson (2001), "Rewards systems have a critical role in determining the organization's ability to attract high potential employees, to retain high performing employees, and to motivate all employees to achieve greater levels of performance" (p. 213). In essence business incentives create opportunities for future and enhanced employment activities.

However, as individual economic values are converted into individual economic incentives and individuals become aligned with respective employers or individuals become employed within an organization, then individual economic value stipends are stopped and become absorbed by the employer. In other words, similar as unemployment benefits cease after becoming employed, individual stipends will cease after becoming employed. Therefore, economic value stipends and incentives serve as temporary measures towards employment infusion. In addition individual economic stipends or subsidies serve to provide a measure of responsibility thereby recognizing that age discriminatory practices does exist regardless of political spectrum, party affiliations, or other organizations.

In the meantime, while attempts to abort discriminatory practices continue, old-age workers continue suffering from discriminatory practices and lack of efficient legal representation. In other words, current employment law practices towards age discrimination are focused on return of investment (ROI) principals rather than stopping discriminatory practices. In essence efficient legal representation should be provided that focuses on resolving discriminatory practices rather than legal business practices or return on investment strategies. Hence, an organization which strengthens the pillars of justice should prevail and take a leading role towards enforcing discriminatory practices. Furthermore, if current laws create deterrents towards equitable justice then laws must be amended ensuring equitable justice.

Unfortunately, legal representation is lacking due to business practices and limited financial barriers. As shown in figure one, individuals communicate his or her discriminatory concerns to his or her individual attorney while company attorney gathers documentation from company human resources. Attorney communication continues or become aborted due to limited financial sources. Furthermore, lack of equitable justice, resolutions, and deterrents creates a legal advantage for company attorneys. As stated by Kapp (2005), "In United States there already exists, on the substantive level, a broad panoply of federal, state, and local statutes, regulations, and judicial precedents directly or indirectly relevant to, and frequently explicitly targeted toward, older persons" (p. 561). As further stated by Giordano (2005), "According to some people, equality does not require us to treat people equally" (p. 83). In essence Jews, African American, women, ethnic groups, or older individuals can be viewed upon and treated differently compared to other individuals.

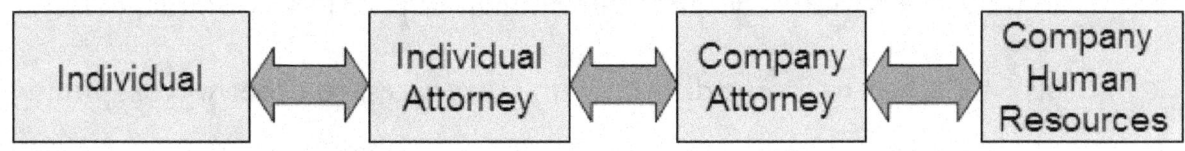

Figure 1

Nonetheless, while justice systems make minimal attempts towards resolving discriminatory practices, other resolutions or opportunities can be developed towards equitable justice. In other words, communication from an employment lawyer stating that "I have been doing this for 35 years" leaves discriminatory justice hanging in unsolved dilemmas. However, pillars of justice can be created, which requires enforcing laws of discriminatory practices. For instance, as shown in figure two, individuals can communicate discriminatory practices with the EEOC and the AARP. In addition the AARP can serve as an individual representative communicating discriminatory concerns to the EEOC.

Thus, effective communication through sufficient evidence and data allows the EEOC to develop probable cause of action. Furthermore, with EEOC and AARP representation, individuals who attempt to protect their rights are not hindered by financial and other retaliatory events.

Consequently, as discriminatory data is determined for probable cause, the EEOC can assign an attorney at an agreed upon rate. In the meantime, a company attorney can gather necessary evidence, make analysis, and come to a reasonable solution. Unfortunately, since discriminatory practices continue, deterrents must be established to thwart discriminatory practices. In other words, punitive damages amounting to triple damages without cap limits towards corporate officers should prevent discriminatory practices. In addition company damages resulting from adverse practices can be used to fund EEOC challenges and provide individual economic relief or individual economic stipends. Thus, community messages from the EEOC will send a signal that discriminatory practices will not be tolerated with economic support provided through the EEOC and the AARP. In essence economic or financial barriers should not be a deterrent for equitable justice in the United States of America (USA). In addition, as stated by Giordano (2005), "Of course, a public policy that is based on the ignorance of the merits, the contribution, and the worth of a group of citizens can neither be accepted nor recommended" (p. 83).

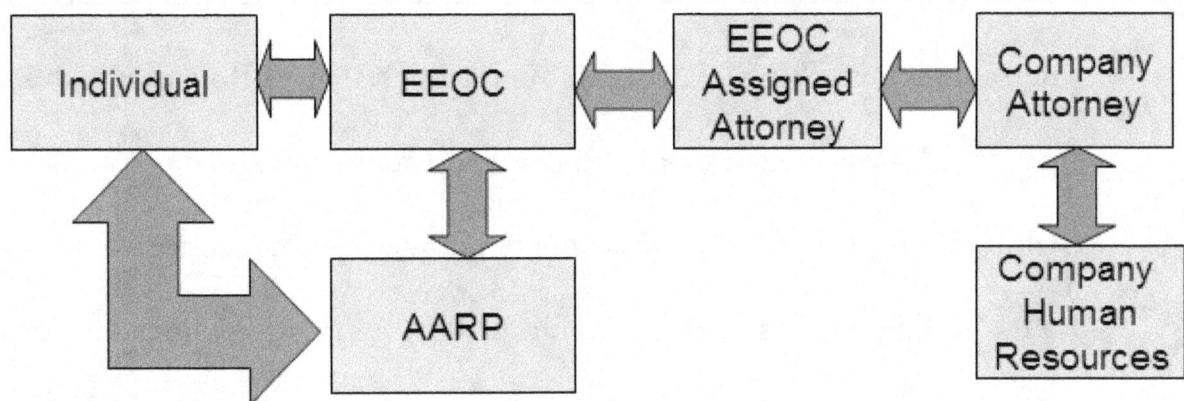

Figure 2

Unfortunately, while discriminatory practices continue, organizations such as the Family Court system contribute to economic calamities and discrimination through workforce misalignment policies. In other words, Family Court processes desire quick employment, which may not be aligned with an individual capabilities or prior work experiences. In addition Family Court processes assume individuals are still employed thus using capable earnings methods. In essence if an individual was earning $3,000 per month during employment then a Family Court process assigns $3,000 per month during periods of unemployment. Therefore, financial calamities combined with a misaligned workforce are developed by a Family Court system and contribute to an existing financial calamity. Furthermore, when multiplying Family Court processes by the number of cases exhibiting periods of employment-to-unemployment then financial calamities become magnified. As stated by Bemiller (2006), "Through their attempts to understand this process,

Neustein and Lesher uncover a corrupt system that abuses its power to the detriment of its clientele" (p. 478). As further stated by Bouchard (2002), "Many people who have had the unfortunate opportunity to experience divorce court from the `receiving' end have wondered how we got the courts we have now" (p. 59). As additionally stated by Shapiro (2005), "I am often knocked over and thrown off course by tidal waves of absolute power, absolute stupidity, and greed" (p. 196). In essence calamities of injustice are contained within a Family Court system, which contributes to an existing economic calamity.

On the other hand, improvements of Family Court laws, which minimize economic calamities, can be developed or becomes a good start. In other words, and as shown in figure three, individual relief within the family court system during periods of unemployment through equitable fairness and reduced expenditures should be established. In essence expenditures or obligations will be held at zero until employment is obtained, which should provide individual economic relief. Furthermore, individuals could become qualified establishing individual economic values or stipends. Additionally, individuals should not be held accountable for economic instability and age discrimination nor be in contempt of court resulting from unemployment, which is causing a deterrent towards becoming employed. Thus, individuals who desire employment, however, are refused employment should not be penalized. As stated by Palm Beach Post

(2004), "Several judges have problems with bias, disregard of due process and heavy-handed treatment of litigants" (p. 15A). As further stated by Guggenheim (2008), "The Family Court is a court that pretends to be helping even when it is harming. And that's what makes it our most dangerous institution" (p. 1). In other words, change, modifications, or an overhaul is essential, which will overcome many Family Court corrupt and discriminatory practices.

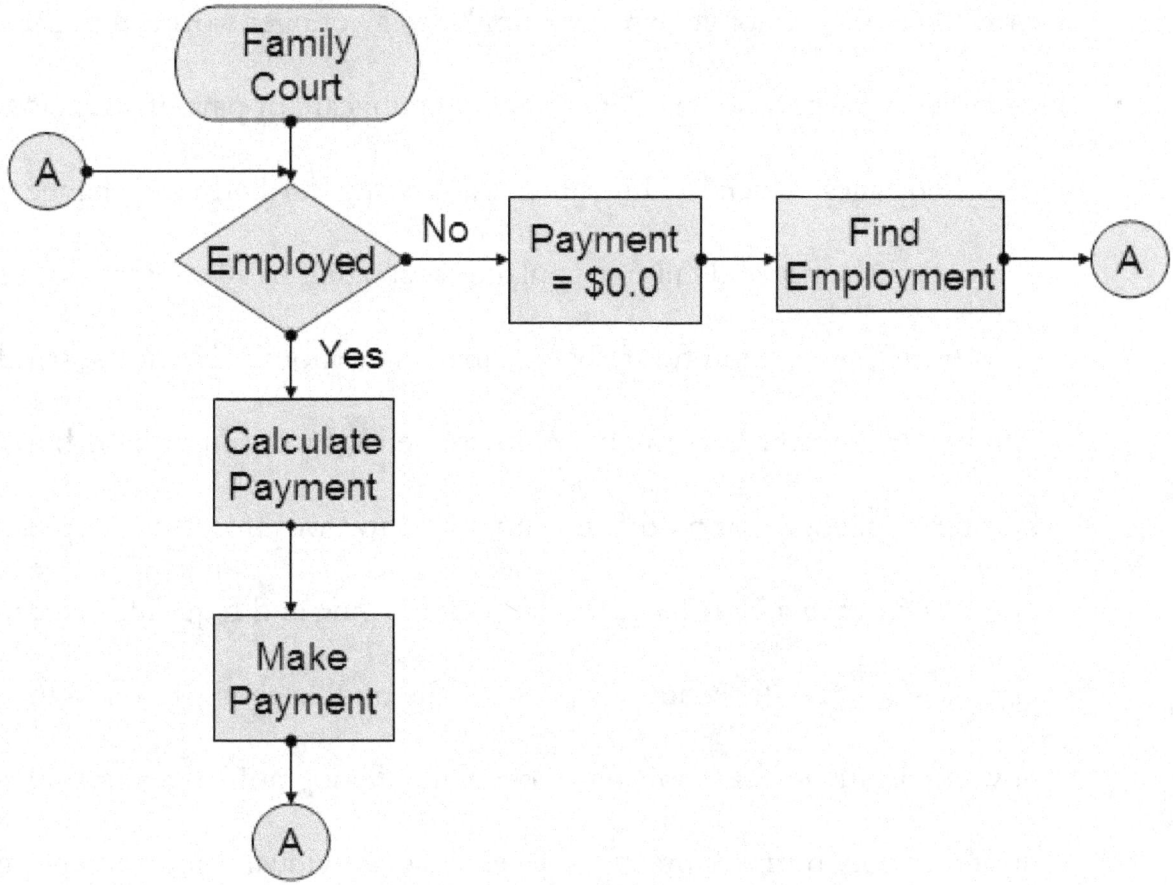

Figure 3

Gap Analysis

The current economy is facing many obstacles, bubbles, and turmoil fueled by changing demographics, a continued aging workforce, and continued company reorganizations. In essence as a baby boomer generation ages, retires from a workforce, or becomes an unwanted individual of society through company reorganizations, then economic dilemmas will result. In other words, an older workforce has economic expenses similar to a younger workforce. Unfortunately, regardless of whom we are democrat or republican, or part of a religious society, everybody ages, which is a human characteristic. Furthermore, change in demographics, rise and fall of populations, creating baby booms and resulting baby busts can result in future baby bangs or economic dilemmas. In addition the number of individuals born after a downsized baby boom or baby burst can not be altered, changed, or modified. Thus, a greater workforce developed by a baby boom is creating a baby bang resulting from aging and requiring economic expenses. Hence, the economic perils of the middle-aged worker being placed in unwanted situations are a result of changing demographics, aging, and adverse discriminatory business practices. In essence individual aging becomes economic turmoil.

Nonetheless, baby boomers began an increased population growth after WWII. As stated by CalculatedRisk (2005), "This is nothing new, but its interesting when considering the debates on Social Security, medical care, budget deficits or when considering investments that are related to demographics (like 2nd homes)" (p. 1). Furthermore, as stated by CalculatedRisk(2005) and shown in figure 4, "The Baby Boom probably peaked in the mid-1950s. The 1960 graph clearly shows both the Baby Bust of the '30s and the Baby Boom that followed" (p. 1). In other words, the aftermath of WWII, economic rebuilding, and restoring family unity created a baby boom and an increased workforce.

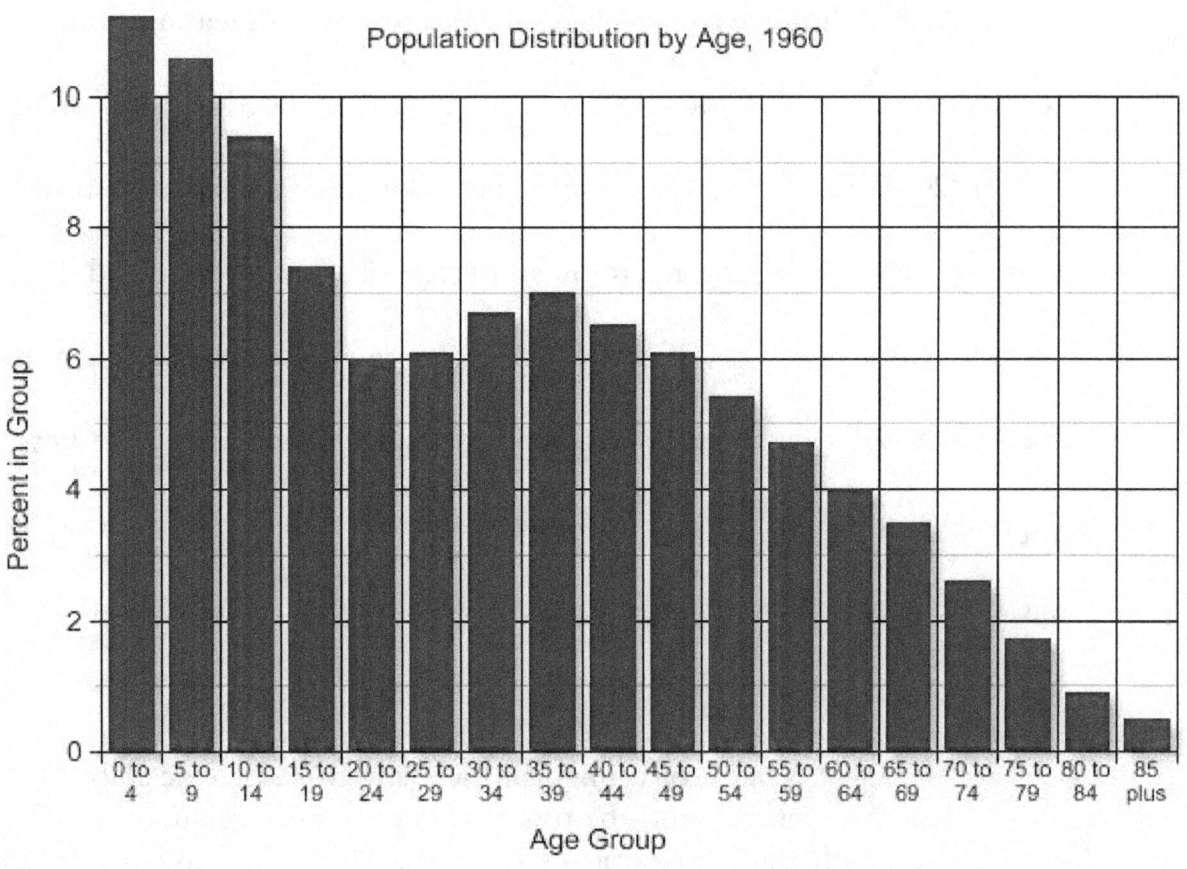

Figue 4, (CalculatedRisk, 2005, p.1).

Nevertheless, the baby boom generation created a massive workforce, approximately 78 million, which ended in 1964. In essence the baby boom generation spanned for 18 years, which has and is approaching the 60 year mark. As stated by Dychtwald and Baxter (2007):

> In the latter decades of the 20th century, organizations enjoyed an abundance of young workers, fueled by the unprecedented baby boom that stretched from 1946 until 1964. In this century, the baby bust that followed the baby boom is creating a critical shortage of younger workers (p. 325).

Thus, a shortage of unskilled younger workers is creating a hiring dilemma for companies seeking younger workers. As further stated by Dychtwald and Baxter (2007), "And yet, the vast majority of organizations persist in recruiting, training, engagement, and retention strategies that were created and designed for a youthful workforce" (p. 325). Therefore, company reorganization is purely focused towards a younger workforce and disregards a matured workers experience and educational achievements. However, as the baby boom generation ages, additional dilemmas are created. As stated by CalculatedRisk (2005) and shown in figure five:

> By 2000 it is hard to distinguish the Baby Bust, but the Baby Boom is very clear. New entries into the population have been relatively steady for years. Even with the lower impact from the Baby Bust, medical costs are still straining the budget - and with the Boomers nearing retirement age, this is clearly a major issue for the US (p. 1).

However, comparing figure four with figure five in the later years discovers an aging population with increased proportions. In other words, an increased population in the later years places additional strains on various systems. Unfortunately, an increased matured population, who has knowledge, skills, education, and desires become an unwanted drain upon society. As stated by Dychtwald and Baxter (2007), "Today, however, with the youngest boomers in their early 40s and the oldest boomers in their early 60s, workforce growth is coming to a virtual standstill" (p. 325). In addition workforce standstill formed through unwanted downsizes creates reduced future social security income adding further dilemmas or retaliations towards a matured workforce.

For instance, as employees gain additional experiences, education, and age through the process, employee's income increases as a result of additional experiences. However, as companies find means to curtail costs, employees with greater incomes normally in an over 40 age bracket find themselves searching for answers or other solutions. As stated by Luhby (2008), "But older workers are increasingly getting the corporate ax these days. Among the unemployed age 55 to 64, nearly 42% had been fired or laid off, up from 32.2% a year ago, according to federal statistics for April" (p. 1). Furthermore, as additionally stated by Luhby (2008), "Many older workers are taking jobs below their pay scale because it's all they can find, said Ward of Seniors4Hire, which is experiencing a greater demand for its services" (p. 1). In addition, as stated by Gover and McClure (2004), "Many companies will not promote older engineers into management, rationalizing that they will not have sufficient years left in their careers for the company to make the investment worthwhile" (p. 1). Similarly, most companies will not hire older individuals resulting from lack of working years remaining thereby creating a continued misalignment of human capital. Therefore, when an aging workforce loses significant income, resulting from unwanted hiring practices or depreciated income on a continual basis, then economic calamities will certainly occur. In other words, significant reduction or loss of income will generate significant reductions in federal, state, social security taxes and other spending revenues, which creates additional losses in foreclosures, credit card, student loan delinquencies, and other social calamities. Thus, social adverse behaviors combined with a decreasing baby boomer workforce will create further calamities if existing policies of ignoring a matured workforce remains.

However, as the baby boomer generation begins the 60 year mark, social and economic calamities will continue resulting from various company reorganizations. As stated by Triest, Sapozhnikov, and Sass (2006), "The United States, along with virtually all other developed countries, is on the cusp of a radical transformation of its labor markets" (p. 4). In essence demographics of the working population is changing, which is producing older workers. As additionally stated by Triest, Sapozhnikov, and Sass (2006), "As a consequence, labor supply may grow at a slower rate than labor demand, putting upward pressure on wages and creating tight labor market conditions" (p. 4). However, often overlooked is a vast supply of older workers, who are capable of performing various employment activities yet who are continuously ignored by hiring companies or agencies.

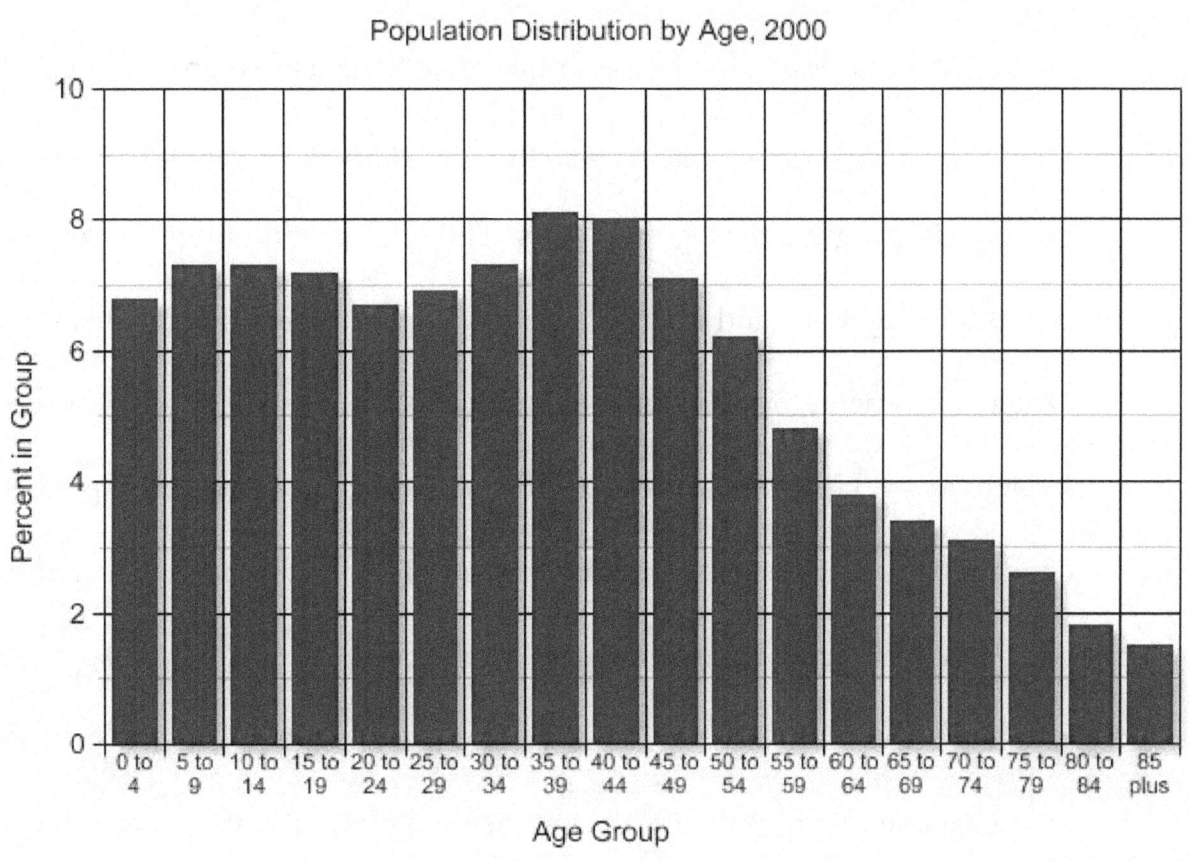

http://calculatedrisk.blogspot.com/

Figure 5 (CalculatedRisk, 2005, p. 1)

Nonetheless, as baby boomers or other generations' age, generations become confronted with waterfall paralysis, which translates into social calamities.

Waterfall paralysis can be defined as a condition occurring resulting from aging where individual experiences, training, or education becomes a no longer desired societies criteria and eventually falls into an area of continued paralysis resulting from corporate downsizing, reorganization, or other disguised withdrawal symptom thereby never to rise or recover again. In essence waterfall paralysis, as shown in figure six, creates social and economic calamities.

Nevertheless, figure six describes the dilemmas that are often faced by middle-aged workers. Figure six displays human capital development as individuals' progress through the years. The vertical and horizontal axis is represented by value and time respectively. For example, as individuals purchase capital equipment, then capital equipment depreciates over time and becomes no longer valued. However, individuals through learning, individual experiences, and education generate increased human capital value. Unfortunately, as individuals age or have obtained excessive human capital, then companies through reorganization find means to depreciate human capital. In other words, as individuals age beyond their 40 years, then various amounts of discriminatory jitter can occur. Discriminatory jitter is described as the various points on the human capital growth curve where waterfall paralysis occurs. In essence a vast discrimination gap exists resulting in discriminatory jitter.

However, while changing demographics resulting in a vast number of middle-aged workers occur, efforts should be focused towards minimizing discriminatory jitter in a workplace. As stated by Triest, Sapozhnikov, and Sass (2006), "…the growth rate of the working age population has already dropped substantially, and … (the ratio of those over 65 to the population aged 15 to 65) will increase dramatically" (p. 4). Thus, as can be seen in figure seven and comparing graphs with figure six, reductions in discriminatory jitter or minimizing waterfall paralysis should be the desired goal. In essence developing individual economic values or stipends, which can be converted to individual economic tax credits, should provide company incentives to re-employ middle-aged workers and prevent or minimize discriminatory jitter. As stated by Dychtwald and Baxter (2007), "As members of the boomer generation enters into their retirement years in greater and greater numbers, organizations will confront a massive brain drain of skills and know-how among their most experienced workers and management" (p. 325). Furthermore, as additionally stated by Dychtwald and Baxter (2007), "Yet, despite the increasing shortage of young workers and the unprecedented growth of available mature workers, organizations continue to focus their recruiting and development efforts on the younger workers" (p. 325). In essence challenges of magnified proportions exist, which will create deterrents towards discriminatory practices and provide opportunities for middle-aged workers to regain valuable presence within the community, the society, and in the workplace.

Nonetheless, continued efforts towards re-employing middle-aged workers should prevail. Since individual aging can not be altered regardless of various disguises employed towards blending with a younger generation, continued efforts should prevail to drive discriminatory jitter out of existence as shown per figure eight. Similarly as African American, Jewish, or other ethnic groups drive discriminatory jitter out of existence, age discrimination should additionally be driven out of existence and restore individuality within a workplace. In addition by shifting the pillars of justice from existent legal organizations whose focus is on return of investment practices to the EEOC or a dedicated organization, can discriminatory practices be minimized and regained control. As stated by Dychtwald and Baxter (2007), "Demographic research, analysis of past employee retirement patterns and surveys of employee retirement intentions and attitudes can help pinpoint risks of employee shortages and prioritize your older worker recruitment and retention strategies" (p. 325). In addition as stated by Jackson (1999), "We are nearly all agreed that justice should be done; but usually we are seriously divided as to what is just in the particular case" (p. 337). Furthermore, overhauling institutions or organizations such as Family Court systems, which contribute towards discriminatory practices and social calamities is gravely

46

warranted. As stated by Lewis (1998), "The city's archaic Family Court system will get a major overhaul designed to reduce the chronic delays that leave children in legal limbo. The announcement follows a campaign by the Daily News to open the Family Courts to public scrutiny" (p. 21). As further stated by Business Editors (1999), "In order to help a family's wounds heal, a timely, fair, efficient, and cost effective means of resolving issues needs to be in place" (p. 1). Unfortunately, a timely, fair, and cost effective family court system is not in place, which further contributes to our society's economic calamity.

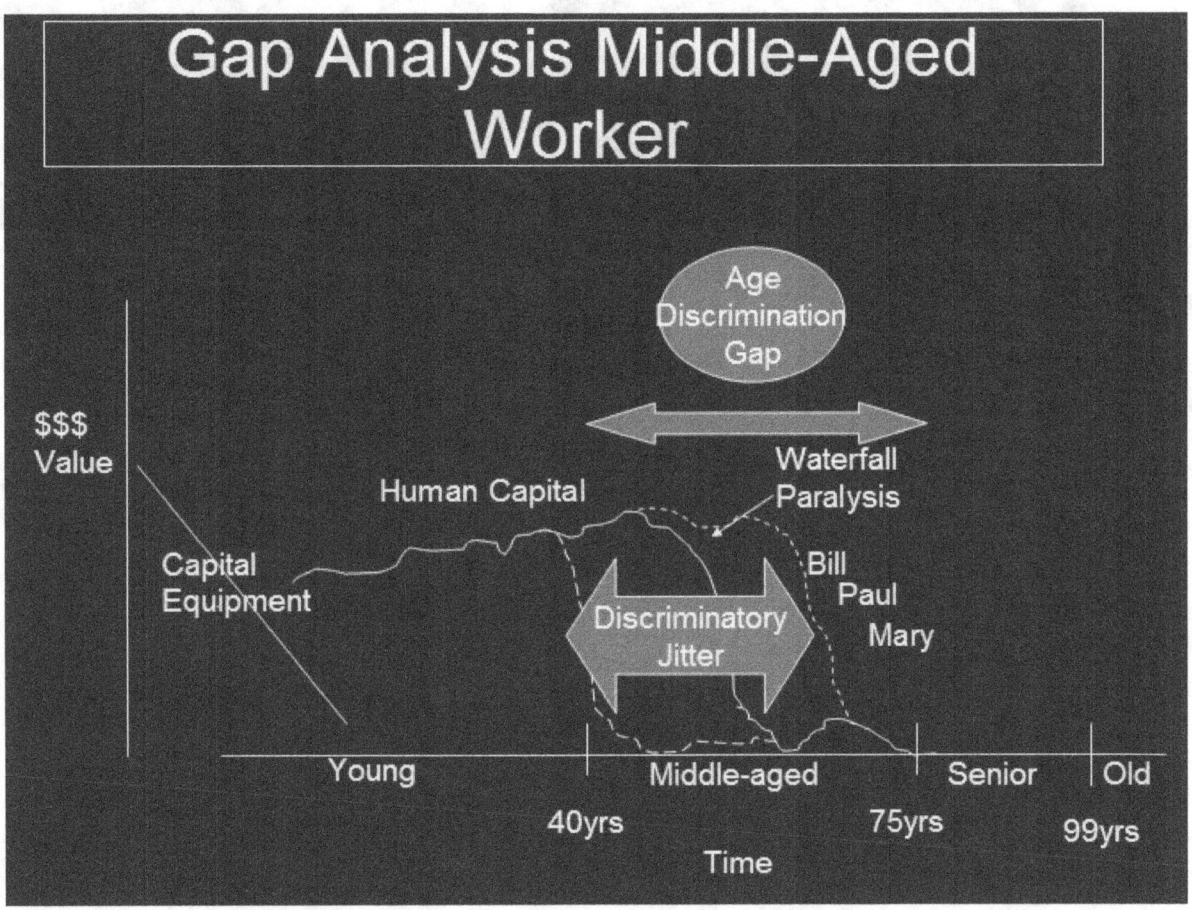

Figure 6 (Johansen, 2008)

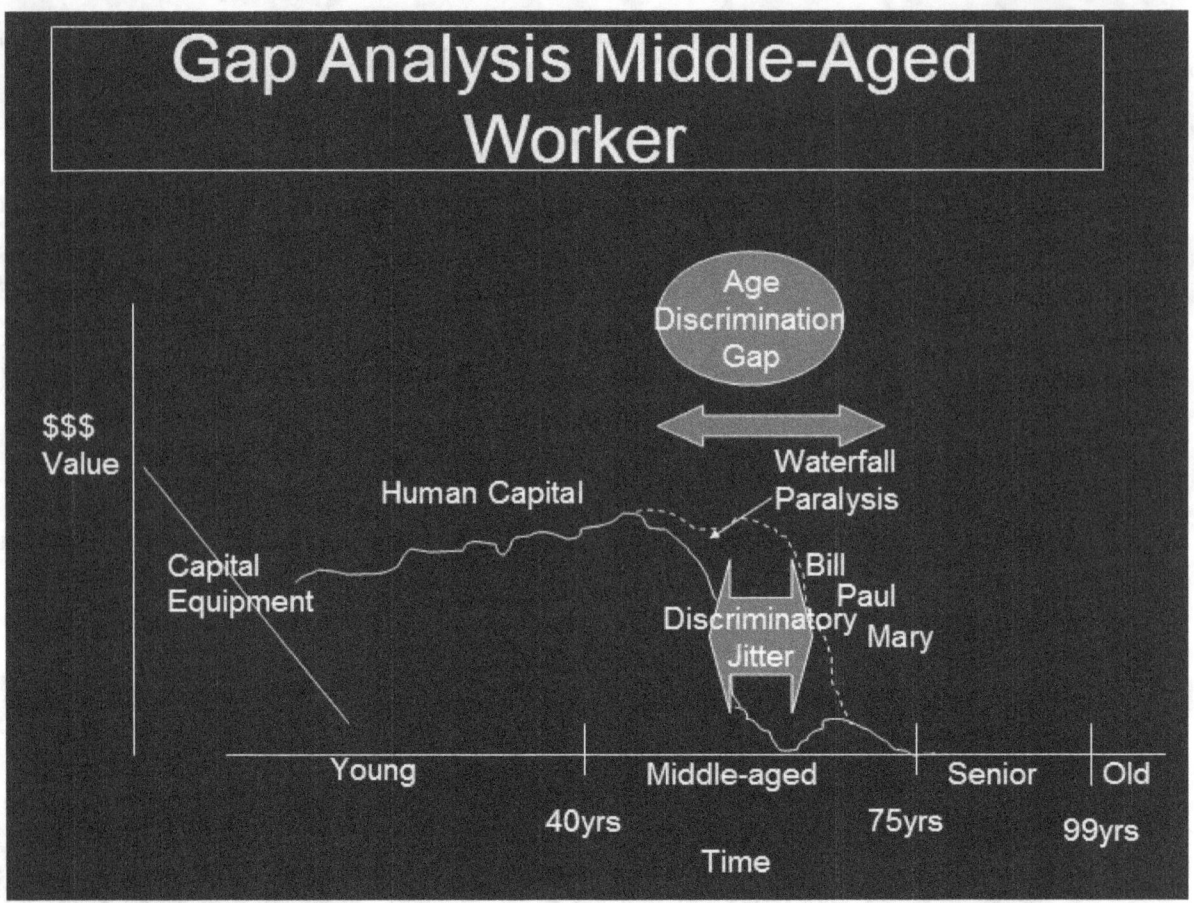

Figure 7 (Johansen, 2008).

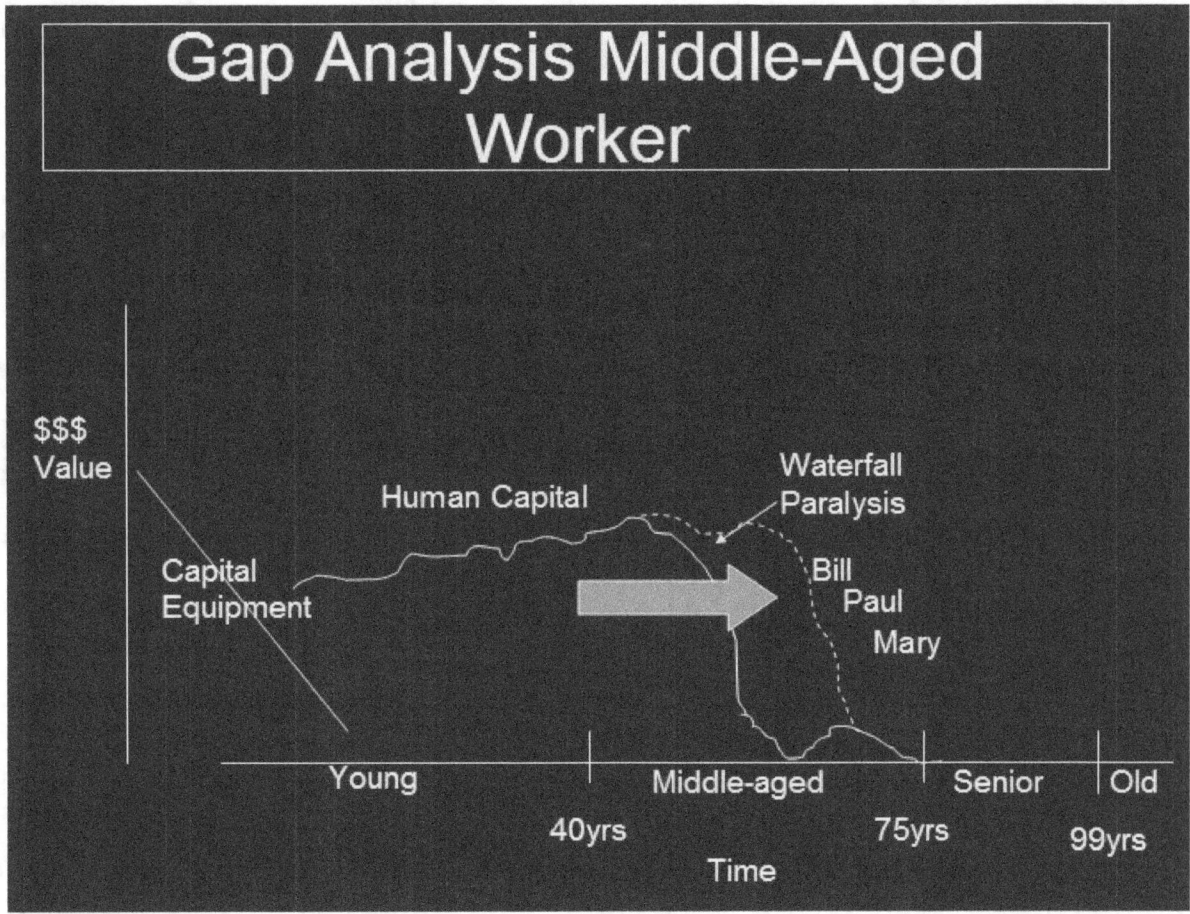

Figure 8 (Johansen, 2008)

Conclusion

Economic perils are encountered daily by middle-aged workers. Continued social behaviors such as myths or workplace traditions create genocidal barriers towards opportunities. In addition, organizations continue adverse practices towards middle-aged workers, which develop into various health dilemmas. Nonetheless, while economic perils or discriminatory practices continue, stakeholders seek equitable fairness and company growth, which contribute towards a GDP equation. Unfortunately, unethical practices create dilemmas for stakeholders and hold organizational leaders accountable.

Thus, as economic perils continue goals or efforts with viable solutions should be sought, which prevents discriminatory practices. Unfortunately, organizations such as family court services, which contribute to economic calamities through job misalignment and continued discriminatory practices require overhauls that mitigate such practices. In essence various discriminatory practices and organizational behaviors create economic calamities.

However, while economic calamities continue, changing demographics resulting from population growth and decline additionally continues. In other words, prior pre-WWII baby burst became baby booms, which was followed by baby bursts. Thus a shortage of babies following the baby boom combined with various discriminatory practices towards middle-aged workers creates a baby bang or economic calamity as is experienced from continued downsized middle-aged workers. In addition continued hiring barriers for middle-aged workers create genocidal effects as experienced by other ethnic groups.

Thus, what the gap analysis provides is how various organizational behaviors towards middle-aged workers develop into calamities resulting from unwanted or discarded practices as continuously experienced by Jews, African-American, or other ethnic groups. In addition continued wide-spread discriminatory jitter through various myths and disguises develops into a waterfall paralysis of global magnitude. However, while various problematic discriminatory conditions exists, opportunities through legal alignment, organizational overhauls, and economic stipends can be developed, which mitigates discriminatory unethical practices towards middle-aged workers who can willingly contribute to an economic society. As stated by Walberg (2007), "Companies that recognize that older people bring many talents and capabilities to the workplace, and find ways to attract them will have a competitive edge" (p. B.8).

Recommendation

While economic calamities continue resulting from changing demographics, discriminatory practices, and organizational or family court contributions, efforts must be incorporated that reflect upon gap analysis visions and mitigate or stop existing practices, which will end economic calamities. In essence as reflected within a gap analysis, recommendations should be incorporated, which will prevent or cease existing discriminatory practices as shown in figure eight. Furthermore, incorporating resulting recommendations that are derived from existing visions will reestablish economic growth through increased hiring, individual respect through recognition of various experiences, employee realignment through individual opportunities, and diminished discriminatory practices resulting from incorporating suggestive recommendations.

1.   Incorporate individual or main street economic values as described in visions, which will establish an individual economic value based upon individual productivity and earnings growth years. In essence focus is directed towards main-street constituents and persons are recognized for individual experiences. Furthermore, similar as individuals are rescued first by individually applying oxygen to oneself during cabin decompression prior to rescuing others in a turmoil, are constituents first rescued that will assist during an economic crisis. However, as individual economic values are calculated using five-year FICA averaged earnings and become short-term individual economic stipends, accountability through employment initiatives or employment reporting will additionally become established. In essence individual economic stipends or stimulus creates individual economic tax credit, which serves as an employer incentive towards hiring motivated career minded individuals. In addition while individual economic stipends are delivered, individual economic stipends become subjected towards various taxes as if individuals are a regular W-2 wage earner. As stated by The New York Times (1989), "Under a program announced by the Board of Education in 1987, pupils in grades 7 through 12 became

eligible for rewards for good marks in their basic courses" (p. A.36). In essence as individuals are rewarded for excellence, companies are rewarded for hiring and recognizing individual capabilities through individual economic tax credits. In addition as companies increase hiring using existing individual economic tax credits, companies are additionally rewarded through decreased business taxes and other incentives. Thus, an infusion of ideas is required, which will meet existing economic challenges.

2.   However, while individual economic stipends require revenue sources towards achieving perspective economic goals, revenue sources can be created and accounts can be established, which will achieve an economic objective. In other words, funding from corporate punitive damages, corporate goodwill, realignment of mismanaged government spending, minimized foreign aid, and other creative strategies will serve as a continued catalyst towards achieving economic growth while mitigating adverse corporate practices. In essence continued government focus towards establishing economic stability by incorporating suggestive methods will mitigate waterfall paralysis through individual recognition.

For instance, corporations receive various punitive damages resulting from vast unethical business practices. As stated by Furniss, Morton, and Harrington (2004), "Again, the Montana Supreme Court affirmed the award because of the bank president's testimony that older employees were 'dead wood' and 'old dead wood.' The banker said at trial that the employee was 'ballast' (p. 14). In essence corporate punitive damages provide funding towards economic growth through individual economic stipends. However, while corporate punitive damages contribute towards economic stability, corporate goodwill through corporate recognition of adverse practices additionally contribute towards economic stability. As stated by Kim (2006):

> In particular, this study highlights why it is important for a corporation to be perceived as a responsible corporate citizen by its target publics in its community, and how and when a company may use various types of message sidedness to make a public relations message more effective, depending on their perceived goodwill and trustworthiness among target publics (p. 1).

Nonetheless, while corporate goodwill contributes towards economic stability, realignment of mismanaged government spending or pork-barrel projects can additionally contribute towards economic stability. In essence misguided projects would be cancelled with allocated funding contributed towards economic stability. As stated by Gaouette (2006), "The accounts of fraud and abuse, along with the Federal Emergency Management Agency's failures during that crisis, have led Congress to demand changes in FEMA" (p. A.20). Therefore, misguided funds or existing pork-barrel spending would be realigned towards achieving economic stability through economic individual stipends. As additionally stated by Frisch, Ph.D. (1997), "This assumption leads some scholars to conclude that the geographic pulls of pork barrel politics results in inefficiency, government growth, and promotes deficit spending" (p. 1).

Nevertheless, while corporate punitive damages, corporate goodwill, and misaligned government projects can contribute towards economic funding, minimized foreign aid through a diversion of allocated funds can additionally contribute towards economic funding. In essence infusions of ideas are essential towards mitigating economic calamities and provide temporary economic assistance to middle-aged or unfortunate main-street employees who are caught in an unexpected economic downturn. As stated by Cox and Duffin (2008), "In the case of foreign economic aid, the cold war's end gives occasion for increasing spending proposals, contrary to the public's expectation that the end of the cold war minimized the need for the U.S. to provide foreign economic assistance" (p. 29). As further stated by Holt (1997), "The foreign-aid bureaucracy, much like the welfare bureaucracy, has acquired a life and momentum of its own" (p. 19). In essence changing foreign aid policies, which divert resources towards main-street economic policies, are essential towards restoring economic stability for main-street employees.

3.   Incorporate economic justice, which prevents discriminatory practices, by establishing pillars of justice as described per figure two. In essence realignment of justice systems from figure one towards figure two would enforce existing discriminatory laws rather than mere façade policies or ROI practices that incorporate Supreme Court Justices intend or outcome. As stated by Benshof (2002), "Only the last two of the four Roe pillars mentioned above remain standing today, a result that is the culmination of a steady decline in constitutional protection for the right to privacy" (p. 12). Therefore, aligning the pillars of justice towards the EEOC, which will enforce or recommend changes of existing discriminatory laws, will mitigate or prevent discriminatory labor practices as currently exhibited in various workplace organizations. Furthermore, as stated by Bush (2005), "In a new century, the alliance of Europe and North America is the main pillar of our security" (p. 290). Similarly, in a new government, the association between EEOC and AARP, will serve as pillars for middle-aged individuals, whose primary mission will be eradicating discriminatory practices. In essence modifications, changes, or alterations are essential towards mitigating discriminatory practices and

economic calamities. As additionally stated by Brownfeld (2002), "Truth, justice and peace, said Rabban Simeon ben Gamaliel, are the three pillars that sustain the world (Avot 1:18)" (p. 87).

4.   Incorporate a Family Court overhaul, which will mitigate or prevent discriminatory and corrupt practices, through investigative processes and Family Court law modifications. In essence identify, modify, or change rulings, which will prevent further contributions of economic instabilities. Thus, implementing processes as identified per figure three and using flow-chart analysis can effectively identify and modify existing legal family court regulations. However, as stated by Brayer, Cookston, and Cohen (2002), "…the legal system generally was thought of by the attorneys (both male and female) to be biased in favor of mothers and against fathers" (p. 325). As further stated by Sexton (1997), "The players themselves acknowledge that the system often works badly or barely works at all, but they differ on where to place the blame. Many judges seem almost not to care what the rules are" (p. 1.1). In essence overhaul of an existing Family Court system is warranted, which contributes towards discriminatory, personal financial, and economic calamities through lack of accountability.

References

Alster, N. (2005). When Gray Heads Roll, Is Age Bias at Work? New York Times, 3.3. Retrieved July 29, 2008, from ProQuest database.

Bemiller, M. (2006). From Madness to Mutiny: Why Mothers Are Running from the Family Courts-and What Can Be Done about It. Contemporary Sociology, 35(5), 478(2). Retrieved November 18, 2008, from ProQuest database.

Benshoof, J. (2002). The Dismantling of Choice. NCJW Journal, 25(1), 12. Retrieved December 9, 2008, from ProQuest database.

Berry, L. L. & Carbone, L. P. (2007). Build Loyalty Through Experience Management. Quality Progress, 40(9), 26(7). Retrieved October 24, 2008, from ProQuest database.

Bouchard, L. J. (2002). Stolen Vows: The Illusion of No-Fault Divorce and the Rise of the American Divorce Industry. Everyman, 57, 59. Retrieved November 18, 2008, from ProQuest database.

Brayer, S. L., Cookston, J. T., & Cohen, B. R. (2002). Experiences of family law attorneys with current issues in divorce practice. Family Relations, 51(4), 325(10). Retrieved December 10, 2008, from ProQuest database.

Brooks, C. (1997). Jesse Jackson urges America to fulfill commitment to further racial justice. New York Amsterdam News, 10. Retrieved November 3, 2008, from ProQuest database.

Brosi, G. & Kleiner, B. H. (1999). Is age a handicap in finding employment. Equal Opportunities International, 18(5/6), 100(5). Retrieved October 23, 2008, from ProQuest database.

Brownfeld, A. C. (2002). The Growing Contradiction Between Jewish Values and the Use of Israeli Power. The Washington Report on Middle East Affairs, 21(4), 87. Retrieved December 9, 2008, from ProQuest database.

Bush, G. W. (2005). Working Together. Vital Speeches of the Day, 71(10), 290(5). Retrieved December 9, 2008, from ProQuest database.

Business Editors (1999). Task Force Report: Revamp Family Court, Says Cohen. Business Wire, 1. Retrieved December 1, 2008, from ProQuest database.

CalculatedRisk (2005). Demographics: Baby Bust and Boom. Retrieved November 23, 2008, from website http://calculatedrisk.blogspot.com/2005/12/demographics-baby-bust-and-boom.html.

CNN Money (2008). Under-employed and under the radar. CNNMoney. Retrieved November 30, 2008, from website http://money.cnn.com/2008/10/03/pf/underemployment/index.htm.

Cox, D. G. & Duffin, D. L. (2008). Cold War, Public Opinion, and Foreign Policy Spending Decisions: Dynamic Representation by Congress and the President. Congress & the Presidency, 35(1), 29(24). Retrieved December 8, 2008, from ProQuest database.

Demsey, A. (2004). Breaking the age barrier. Irish Times, 13. Retrieved July 24, 2008, from ProQuest database.

Dychtwald, K. & Baxter, D. (2007). Capitalizing on the New Mature Workforce. Public Personnel Management, 36(4), 325(10). Retrieved November 23, 2008, from ProQuest database.

Fay, C. H. & Thompson, M. A. (2001). Contextual determinants of reward systems' success: An exploratory study. Human Resource Management, 40(3), 213. Retrieved November 17, 2008, from ProQuest database.

Frank, B., Forbes, S., Soros, G., and Brittan, S. et al (2004). Who Should Be the Next Fed Chairman? The International Economy, 18(4), 44(7). Retrieved November 10, 2008, from ProQuest database.

Frisch, S. A., Ph.D. (1997). An empirical study of congressional appropriations earmarks. The Claremont Graduate University. Retrieved December 8, 2008, from ProQuest database.

Furniss, J., Morton, J., & Harrington, M. (2004). Punitive Damages. Montana Business Quarterly, 42(2), 14(4). Retrieved December 7, 2008, from ProQuest database.

Gaouette, N. (2006). Panel Criticizes Homeland Security Deals; A report says that amid a surge in spending, $34.3 billion in contracts were mismanaged. Los Angeles Times. Retrieved December 8, 2008, from ProQuest database.

Gerry, B. (2008). AGE REALLY IS JUST A STATE OF MIND. Spokesman Review, PF.4. Retrieved October 30, 2008, from ProQuest database.

Gibson, K. J., Zerbe, W. J., & Franken, R. E. (1993). Employers perceptions of the re-employment barriers faced by older job hunters. Relations Industrielles, 48(2), 321(14). Retrieved October 26, 2008, from ProQuest database.

Giordano, S. (2005). Respect for equality and the treatment of the elderly: Declarations of human rights and age-based rationing. Cambridge Quarterly of Healthcare Ethics, 14(1), 83(10). Retrieved November 17, 2008, from ProQuest database.

Gleason, M. (2007). Lecturer warns of changing workplace. Bennington Banner, 1. Retrieved July 27, 2008, from ProQuest database.

Gover, J. & McClure, G. (2004). The Realities of Age Discrimination. IEEE-USA

Today's Engineer Online. Retrieved October 26, 2008, from website

http://www.todaysengineer.org/2004/Feb/age-discrimination.asp

Graham, G. (1996). Author Says Myths, Not Seniors, Should Be Forced Into

Retirement. The Salt Lake Tribune, F.1. Retrieved November 2, 2008, from

ProQuest database.

Grant, L. D. (1996). Effect of ageism on individual and health care providers'

responses to healthy aging. Health & Social Work, 21(1), 9. Retrieved

November 12, 2008, from ProQuest database.

Guggenheim, M. (2008). Family Court Assailed As Overprotective On Crime.

New York University. Retrieved November 19, 2008, from website

http://query.nytimes.com/gst/fullpage.html?res=9407E2DA133BF932A3

5750C0A964948260&sec=health&spon=&pagewanted=2

Holt, P. M. (1997). Like Welfare, Foreign Aid Shouldn't Go on Endlessly.

Christian Science Monitor, 19. Retrieved December 8, 2008, from

ProQuest database.

Hyde, J. (2008). Polish Jew gave his life defining, fighting genocide.

CNN.com/Europe. 1. Retrieved December 1, 2008, from website

http://www.cnn.com/2008/WORLD/europe/11/13/sbm.lemkin.profile/

index.html

Jackson, K. B. (1999). Economic Justice. Social Theory and Practice, 25(2), 337(7). Retrieved November 24, 2008, from ProQuest database.

Johnson, P. R., Indvik, J., & Rawlins, C. (2007). WILL YOU STILL LOVE ME WHEN I'M 64? THE BOOMERS AT WORK. Allied Academies International Conference. Academy of Organizational Culture, Communications and Conflict Proceedings, 12(2), 15(7). Retrieved October 29, 2008, from ProQuest database.

Kapp, M. B. (2005). Elders on Trial: Age and Ageism in the American Legal System. The Gerontologist, 45(4), 561(3). Retrieved November 17, 2008, from ProQuest database.

Kennedy, A. (2008). National Institute of Anxiety and Stress. Retrieved July 24, 2008 from e-mail database.

Kim, J. R., Ph.D. (2006). An experimental test of public relations messages: Sidedness, and corporate goodwill and trustworthiness. University of Florida. Retrieved December 8, 2008, from ProQuest database.

Lander, G. H. & Reinstein, A. (2005). Corporate Governance and Economic Value Alignment. International Advances in Economic Research, 11(4), 433. Retrieved November 16, 2008, from ProQuest database.

Laskey, J. (2008). Fight Age Discrimination, Stay Positive. Everyday Health. Retrieved November 13, 2008, from website http://www.everydayhealth.com/longevity/emotional-wellness/fighting-age-discrimination.aspx.

Lawson, D. M. C. Ph.D. (2005). The effect of wage discrimination on privileged groups. University of Notre Dame, 139. Retrieved November 10, 2008, from ProQuest database.

Lewis, D. L. (1998). REDESIGN TO SPEED FAMILY COURT CASES. New York Daily News, 21. Retrieved December 1, 2008, from ProQuest database.

Luhby, T. (2008). Out of a job and out of luck at 54. CNN Money. Retrieved November 23, 2008, from website http://money.cnn.com/2008/05/21/news/economy/olderworkers/index.htm?postversion=2008052109

Marshall, V. M. (2007). Advancing the Sociology of Ageism. Social Forces, 86(1), 257(8). Retrieved November 11, 2008, from ProQuest database.

Martinez, O. R. & Kleiner, B. H. (1993). Discrimination in employment by age. Equal Opportunities International, 12(5), 1-5. Retrieved July 29, 2008, from ProQuest database.

McConnell 7 Brue (2004). Economics, 16th Edition. New York: The McGraw-Hill Companies. Retrieved November 10, 2008, from the University of Phoenix e-book collection.

New York Times (1989). FOLLOW-UP ON THE NEWS; Paying cash For
School Grades. Retrieved December 7, 2008, from ProQuest database.

O'Boyle, E. J. (2001). Salary compression and inversion in the university
workplace. International Journal of Social Economics, 28(10-12), 959(21).
Retrieved November 16, 2008, from ProQuest database.

Orr, D. (2004). Courts, children and a litany of flawed judgments; There is a real
sense in which the family courts are not at all interested in justice, or even
fairness. The Independent, 21. Retrieved October 27, 2008, from ProQuest
database.

Osborne, T. & McCann, L. A. (2008). Forced Ranking and Age-Related
Employment Discrimination. Human Rights Magazine. Retrieved October
26, 2008, from website

http://www.abanet.org/irr/hr/spring04/forced.html.

Overell, S. (2005). Age-old question of bias. Personnel Today, 8. Retrieved
November 16, 2008, from ProQuest database.

Palm Beach Post (2004). Pariente Correct: Family Courts Need An Overhaul.
Palm Beach Post, 15A. Retrieved November 19, 2008, from ProQuest
database.

Paul, R. J. & Townsend, J. B. (1993). Managing the older worker – Don't just rinse away the gray. The Academy of Management Executive, 7(3), 67(8). Retrieved October 24, 2008, from ProQuest database.

Peacock, L. (2007). Help the Aged charity calls for anti-age discrimination laws to be extended to cover public services. Personneltoday. Retrieved November 13, 2008, form website

http://www.personneltoday.com/articles/2007/09/03/42174/help-the-aged-charity-calls-for-anti-age-discrimination-laws-to-be-extended-to-cover-public-services.html.

Phipps, F. M. (2006). Is ageism the acceptable face of discrimination?; Changing the attitude toward older workers. Managerial Law, 48(6), 521. Retrieved October 29, 2008, from ProQuest database.

Rasche, H. L. (2006). Actresses, age, and anxiety: A study of midlife women in the film and television industry. University of California, Santa Barbara, 1-178. Retrieved July 28, 2008, from ProQuest database.

Reality doesn't back myths of older workers. (1992). Edmonton Journal, C.9. Retrieved October 30, 2008, from ProQuest database.

Report By Chief Justice's Commission Laments Low Funding For Legal Services As A Denial Of Access To Justice (2008). N.C. Access to Justice

Commission. Retrieved October 26, 2008, from website

http://www.ncbar.org/featuredItems/1/3047/index.aspx.

Rogers, H. P. Ogbuehi, A. O., & Kochunny, C. M. (1995). Ethics and transnational corporations in developing countries: A social contract perspective. Journal of Euro – Marketing, 4(2), 11(28). Retrieved November 10, 2008, from ProQuest database.

Ryan, E. B., Szechtman, B, & Bodkin, J. (1992). Attitudes Toward Younger and Older Adults Learning to Use Computers. Journal of Gerontology, 47(2), 96(6). Retrieved November 12, 2008, from ProQuest database.

Schulz, A. J., Gravlee, C. C., Williams, D. R., and Israel, B. A., et al (2006). Discriminations, Symptoms of Depression, and Self-Rated Health Among African American Women in Detroit: Results From a Longitudinal Analysis. Journal of Public Health, 96(7), 1265(6). Retrieved November 11, 2008, from ProQuest database.

Scott, F. A., Berger, M. C., & Garen, J. E. (1995). Do health insurance and pension costs reduce the job opportunities for older workers? Industrial & Labor Relations Review, 48(4), 775(17). Retrieved July 25, 2008, from ProQuest database.

Sexton, J. (1997). Opening the Doors on Family Court's Secrets. New York Times, 1.1. Retrieved December 10, 2008, from ProQuest database.

Shapiro, L. (2005). Can She Do That? Berkeley Journal of Gender, Law & Justice, 20, 196(3). Retrieved October 27, 2008, from ProQuest database.

Shearring, H. A. (1992). Creativity and Older Adults. Leadership & Organization Development Journal, 13(2), 11(6). Retrieved November 2, 2008, from ProQuest database.

Triest, R. K., Sapozhnikov, M., & Sass, S. A. (2006). Population Aging And The Structure Of Wages. Center for Retirement Research at Boston College, 30. Retrieved November 24, 2008, from website http://escholarship.bc.edu/cgi/viewcontent.cgi?article=1114&context=retirement_papers

Tudway, R. & Pascal, A.M. (2006). Corporate governance, shareholder value and societal expectations. Corporate Governance, 6(3), 305. Retrieved November 10, 2008, from ProQuest database.

Tuitions soar yet law schools offer students little relief. (2000). Michigan Chronicle, 64(10), B10. Retrieved October 26, 2008, from ProQuest database.

United States Department of Justice (2008). Discrimination in Housing Based Upon Race or Color. Civil Rights Division. Retrieved November 3, 2008, from website http://www.usdoj.gov/crt/housing/housing_coverage.php.

University of Phoenix (2008). Gap Analysis. Retrieved November 16, 2008, from

the University of Phoenix website.

Vidal, B. (2006). Ethics and Fair Treatment, a business growth strategy? Colorado

Company, 3. Retrieved November 10, 2008, from website

http://209.85.173.104/search?q=cache:gzdsPERvofsJ:www.employerservi

cesgroup.com/documents/Article-

BusinessEthicsr.pdf+ethics+creates+growth&hl=en&ct=clnk&cd=5&gl=

us&client=firefox-a.

Walberg, M. (2007). Age bias persists in the workplace. The Times – Transcript,

B.8. Retrieved November 2, 2008, from ProQuest database.

Woolnough, R. (2004). Experienced staff earn less money. Personnel Today, 4.

Retrieved July 29, 2008, from ProQuest database.

Table 1

Issue and Opportunity Identification

Issue	Opportunity	Reference to Specific Course Concept (Include citation)	Concept
An individual who appears old, no matter how much work or effort that has been placed within the company, your talents, trust, and organizational fit is no longer required. In essence, your portrayed image or skills are no longer required due to visual appearance.

Furthermore, creating obscure walls or barriers to opportunity because of one's age develops unjustified barriers to individuals who desire continued personal growth. | Barriers to opportunities create challenges. Similarly, as the Berlin wall came down, the barrier walls to opportunity must come down. In essence, the middle-aged worker desires personal growth, opportunity, and not be placed in an unwanted, unfit, or mythical job position. | "…loyalty, dependability, flexibility, trust, and putting in long hours (with absolutely no expectation for additional compensation or recognition) were no longer important" (Kennedy, 2008).

"Stereotyping older people damages us all. First, it can mean we overlook the resources, skills and experiences which older people place at our disposal" (Dempsey, 2004, p. 13). | Age becomes a barrier to opportunity |
| There is an assumption that health care costs for the older worker | Hiring decisions should not be | "Since older workers are more costly to insure, | Health insurance costs create barriers to hiring |

70

will be greater than the younger workers. In essence there is a health-care cost-to-cost comparison, which effects a hiring decision. Furthermore, health care insurance costs for the older worker are greater than for a younger worker, which crates reduced opportunities for employment. In essence presumed older worker health-care costs create a deterrent to hire older workers.	based on health costs rather than on individual capabilities. In essence can an individual perform the specific job? Does the individual have the necessary skill sets to perform the task? Thus, hiring decisions should be based on skill-sets, capabilities, and educational knowledge rather than health-care costs of an individual.	their labor market opportunities relative to those of younger workers may be substantially reduced. Given these cost differences, it is reasonable to hypothesize that health insurance can be an important consideration in a firm's decision to hire older workers" (Scott, Berger, & Garen, 1995, p. 775). "In the next 10 to 15 years, scientists will be able to predict who is more likely to get certain diseases," Meyer said. "This information will likely influence hiring, and that's a major concern at the federal level" (Gleason, 2007, p. 1)	decisions.
Employment training agencies suggest limiting years on a resume. In other words, the resume is disguised	Hiring decisions should not be based on individual	"…does erasing the signs of age on the female face undermine an actress's work and	Individual appearance creates barriers to employment.

to show minimal working experiences, thereby disguising individual age. Furthermore, additional disguises through plastic surgery, cosmetic surgery, or hair modifications are required to create a younger look. In essence, the employer seeks a younger person to fulfill the job role, which requires an older worker to make distinguishable changes.	appearance rather than on individual capabilities. In essence can an individual perform the specific job? Does the individual have the necessary skill sets to perform the task? Thus, hiring decisions should be based on skill-sets, capabilities, and educational knowledge rather than on appearance of an individual.	challenge the autonomy of her performance? These actresses, who agreed to be interviewed only under the protection of anonymity, say they experience a "menopausal blackout," a lack of employment at midlife that suggests gendered ageism" (Rasche, 2006, p. 1) "Companies want to promote an image of a young, mobile staff. 'We are a young company of young people'" (Brosi & Kleiner, 1999, p. 100).	
Employers assume that older workers demand higher salaries. In essence, employers disrespect the education and experience of older workers. Thus, an assumption exists that older workers produce less value than a younger worker.	Employers have an opportunity to recognize that human capital improvements consist of personal experiences, training, educational pursuits,	"Another reason, he said, is that there is often an economic incentive for companies to shed older workers. Those workers tend to earn more and have higher health costs, and their family ties can make them less	Middle-aged disrespectfulness towards human capital improvements

Similarly, a female worker produces less value than a male worker. Thus, employers assume older workers should earn less than younger worker, which is similar to female workers, should earn less than male workers.	sacrifices, and other life experiences. Furthermore, human capital improvements have values that increase similar as individuals pursue higher learning. However, individuals should not be treated as depreciating assets, which can be written off as an invaluable commodity.	flexible about work hours, business travel and relocations. The suit also contends that younger workers were more likely than their older colleagues to receive training that led to promotions and raises" (Alster, 2005, p. 3.3). "Experience is no longer the most valuable commodity for the HR professional, with the majority of over-50s earning less than their younger counterparts. Industry experts believe employers are more concerned about the recruitment and retention of younger employees, and are therefore prepared to pay them inflated bonuses and higher salary increases" (Woolnough, 2004, p. 1).	
Employers assume	Employers	"Many managers or	Attitude

older workers have an attitude problem, which creates difficulty in a working environment. Thus, employers develop unproven myths and create an environment not inductive for the middle-aged worker. In essence the working environment created by an organization can change individual behaviors, which causes the organization to blame the middle-aged worker for their behavior.	have an opportunity to show respect and stop unwanted myths by creating environments of person-based structures. Furthermore, recognizing that employees within an organization are customers within organization changes attitudes that develop person-based structures.	personnal offices have the attitude that the older workforce is less productive or capable in performing their day-to-day activities. Most of the discrimination of older workers appears to be based on myths about performance, reliability, and attendance, instead of reality" (Martinez & Kleiner, 1993, p. 1). "Organizations must think far more deeply about customers' emotional needs and understand how the consistency and effectiveness of clues evoke the emotions that create their customers' experiences of the company" (Berry & Carbone, 2007, p. 26).	stereotypes, myths, or false impressions create barriers or handicaps to opportunities.
Employers assume older workers use	Employers have an	"Psychologists have sought for years to	Middle-aged workers receive

outdated methods. In essence, the employer is biased towards younger workers and assumes older workers are not capable of learning new methods. Thus, an older worker is refrained from learning new company skills.	opportunity to recognize older workers or middle-aged workers have capabilities in learning new skills or trades similar as so-called younger workers.	disprove the widespread belief that older people are unable to learn new skills. Their capacity to learn new things is not much less than that of younger people. Not only do they have the ability but they also have the desire to learn" (Paul & Townsend, 1993, p. 67). "The older job hunter is seen as technologically obsolete. More than half of the responses in this category concerned the perception that older job hunter's 'have a poor education', 'lack the appropriate training' and are 'stuck in their trade' (Gibson, Zerbe, & Franken, 1993, p. 321).	barriers towards training creating company incapable training myths
Discrimination through company reorganization and age hiring dilemmas fuels various forms of social problems such as	Opportunities can be developed, which eliminate age discrimination	"Perceived discrimination can have consequences in its own right, affecting health, well-being and	Discrimination creates depression, which fuels anxiety and other social

depression, anxiety, or divorce. In essence age discrimination symptoms as encountered by African American or the Jewish population create similar dilemmas for old-age skilled workers. Furthermore discriminatory behaviors towards an older work force create mental and physical problems similar as encountered by other minority populations.	resulting in improvements towards social and mental health well being. In essence an older worker can be a productive member of society, which can improve his or her personal stigma.	occupational behavior" (Marshall, 2007, p. 257). "…everyday encounters with discrimination are causally associated with poor mental and physical health outcomes" (Schulz, Gravlee, Williams, Israel, et al, 2006, p. 1265).	dilemmas
Employees find limited recourse towards unwanted hiring, involuntary layoff, or other labor law violations due to limited financial resources. In essence, limited money resources prevent discoveries and equitable justice resolutions. Thus, an employee 'throws in the towel' due to lack of financial or other reasonable resources.	Opportunities for equitable and reasonable justice should become available for all individuals. In essence establishing methods for equitable justice could create deterrents to law violations. Furthermore, individuals should not be cornered into unwanted decisions such as payments for rent or legal	"…surmounting barriers to equal justice that affect millions of low-income individuals and families" (Michigan Chronicle, 2000, p. B10). "The report decried the lack of adequate legal representation for people in poverty who found themselves involved in civil litigation in which critical legal matters such as child custody, eviction, employment, and	Financial handicaps create barriers to equitable justice.

	services.	others were being decided by the courts" (Equal Access to Justice Commission, 2008, p. 1).	
Employers find different methods, loop holes, or disguises towards age discrimination, which create challenges for the middle-aged workers. In other words employers will proceed at great lengths to hide or disguise any discriminatory issues.	Opportunities exists that removes loop holes or other discriminatory dilemmas. Similarly as the African American fought continuously to remove the stigma of racial discrimination, individuals should establish opportunities, which remove the disguises of discrimination.	"Salary curves typically show corporate engineers' salaries declining after age 45. Companies often go to great lengths to disguise this obvious discriminatory practice" (Gover & McClure, 2004, p. 1). "In cases such as *Ford, Goodyear,* and *Capital One,* forced ranking was alleged to have been a purposeful disguise for intentional age discrimination. For example, the *Siegel* plaintiffs charged that Ford's forced ranking process 'was designed and implemented to eliminate through involuntary separation or	Discriminatory practices through clever disguises.

		constructively discharge its older employees'" (Osborne & McCann, 2008, p. 1)	
Organizations such as Family Court create barriers to opportunity by creating individual misalignments that satisfy family court issues rather than individual endeavors. In other words family court is not interested in aligning an individual with respective positions rather than meeting current family court agenda.	Opportunities are encouraged in the family court system, which will minimize employee alignment through equitable fairness. In other words individuals should not be burdened undo pressures due to economic and age handicap dilemmas while another party awaits compensation.	"For many people, the family courts have been a problem for years. The power they have is more absolute in some ways than the criminal courts" (Orr, 2004, p. 21). "I am often knocked over and thrown off course by tidal waves of absolute power, absolute stupidity, and greed" (Shapiro, 2005, p. 196).	Organizations such as Family Courts create barriers to opportunity

Table 2

Stakeholder Perspectives

Stakeholder Perspectives	
Stakeholder Groups	**The Interests, Rights, and Values of Each Group**
United States government	The United States government seeks growth, stability, and economic fairness, which creates gradual increases in the Gross Domestic Product (GDP). However, creating economic fairness requires a workforce that is aligned within their capabilities, which can strengthen an existing workforce.
United States corporations	United States corporations seek growth through investments that contribute towards shareholders through increased share values and growth towards the GDP. However, achieving goals towards GDP and shareholder value requires equitable fairness and corporate ethics. In essence through ethics and regulatory compliances can United States corporations achieve gradual growth of the GDP.
United States shareholders	United States shareholders seek growth in shareholder value. However, shareholders seek growth through equitable fairness and ethical behavior. In essence shareholders desire increased shareholder growth through corporate ethics and regulatory compliance.

Table 3

End State Goals

End-State Goals
1. Stop old age discrimination created by disguised company reorganizations and delayed hiring practices through developing an economic individual value system. In essence respect towards aged individuality recognizing personal achievements, education, and training has an economic value not related as a depreciating asset.
2. Restore equitable value of the old age workers through converting economic values into economic tax credits. In essence economic tax credits serve as an incentive to hire individuals and generate accountability through ethical reporting. In addition similar as bank interest rates are reduced to encourage borrowing, business income taxes should be further reduced to encourage hiring. Thus, combined efforts through individual tax credits and reduced business taxes provide encouragement toward hiring older capable workers.
3. Provide efficient legal representation that focuses on resolving discriminatory practices rather than business practices or return on investment strategies. In essence an organization which undermines the pillars of justice should prevail and take the leading role towards enforcing discriminatory practices. Furthermore, if current laws create deterrents towards equitable justice then laws must be amended ensuring equitable justice.
4. Provide individual relief within the family court system during periods of unemployment through equitable fairness and reduced expenditures. In essence expenditures will be held at zero until employment is obtained, which should provide individual economic relief. Thus obligations will be held at zero for the duration of unemployment. In addition individuals should not be held accountable for economic instability and age discrimination, which is causing a deterrent towards becoming employed. Individuals who desire employment, however are refused employment should not be penalized.

A Blank Page

The Forgotten Graveyard Worker

Peter H Johansen, MBA/HRM

May 7, 2009

The Forgotten Graveyard Worker

Companies are ever confronted by economic challenges addressing shareholder demands while seeking competitive advantages in a global environment. Meeting such competitive advantages and evolved through the industrial revolution required companies efficiently managing fixed and human capital resources. In essence establishment of light-at-night capabilities provided companies with 24/7 or continuous operation. In addition establishment of night-at-light capabilities enabled increased manufacturing capabilities, while reducing effective manufacturing costs.

However, while light-at-night capabilities provided company competitive advantages, light-at-night perils created company calamities resulting from light-at-night conditions. In other words, light-at-night company operations create human challenges resulting from non-standard working conditions. As stated by Han (2007), "The US Census reports that about 15% of the workforce (approximately 15 million people) work evenings, nights, rotating shifts, or irregular schedules or hours (US Bureau of Labor Statistics, 2005)" (p. 1). As further stated by Han (2007), "The transformation of jobs to serve the needs of a global 24-7 economy is having profound effects on work, workers, and their families" (p. 1). In essence as companies use light-at-night advantages towards improved company operations, light-at-night company advantages create long-term individual perils resulting from light-at-night conditions.

Thus, what this paper describes, how light-at-night conditions contribute towards depression, anxiety, divorce, cancer, or other domino symptoms, which encompass an abundance of graveyard calamities. Furthermore, while graveyard employees or stakeholders attempt towards achieving company objectives, graveyard employees can be treated as sub-humans, afterthoughts, expendable human capital, scapegoats, or other indigenous individuals created by management behavior. However, while stakeholders, being employees, upper management, or shareholders desire ethical working conditions, upper management through unethical practices of graveyard calamities will sacrifice short-term profits for individual perils.

Nevertheless, while end-state visions develop futuristic developments towards overcoming graveyard calamities, end-state visions create additional opportunities towards mitigating graveyard calamities. In essence alternative resolutions are warranted towards minimizing graveyard calamities, while creating a productive and family-valued workforce. Nonetheless, as individuals seek protective rights towards health and safety, "GODless" companies, on the other hand, discover disguises towards mitigating individual rights.

Situation Analysis

Issue and Opportunity Identification

Society is ever being challenged towards efficient manufacturing operations and processes. In addition companies seek maximum productivity using fixed and human capital towards company's greatest potential. In essence companies identify creative means towards continued and continuous proficient operations. Therefore, accomplishing efficient continuous company operations requires uninterrupted or 24/7 operations. Unfortunately, while uninterrupted operations are a desired goal, uninterrupted operations created by adverse working conditions develops human challenges, which are compromised through company operations. As stated by Randall (2003), "The 24/7 economy may look profitable on paper, but not if potential profits are eaten by lawsuits and skyrocketing insurance premiums" (p. 1). In essence a 24/7 economy can have detriments towards efficient company operations.

Nevertheless, accomplishing continuous plant operations requires various shift work activities. In essence individuals are operating during day, mid, night shift, or graveyard conditions. Unfortunately, while individuals are operating during night shift or graveyard conditions, individuals develop night-shift depression resulting from out-of-sync biological clock operations. In essence being employed on a graveyard shift creates alienation resulting from loss of societies networks. As stated by Jackson (2005), "You suffer from depression because you don't see the sun ... you have personal conflicts within your family; it can cause loneliness, depression, substance abuse when people use (chemicals such as medication or alcohol) to get to bed ..." (p. 1). Furthermore, as additionally stated by Perry-Jenkins, Goldberg, Pierce, and Sayer (2007), "Results suggest that for new parents, working nonday shifts may be a risk factor for depressive symptoms and relationship conflict" (p. 123). In essence while companies seek maximum profits through efficient operations, companies are developing a night-shift depressed society resulting from night-shift or graveyard operation.

Nonetheless, while night-shift depression is being developed in company workplaces, companies have an opportunity or responsibility towards a workforce by reducing night-shift or graveyard depression. In other words, opportunities can be developed through awareness and company quality improvements, which will minimize night-shift depression resulting from an alienated and grave workforce. As stated by Allday (2008), "...the graveyard shift has been associated with everything from ulcers and depression to heart disease and cancer" (p. 1). In essence night-shift depression is real, which must be taken seriously.

Nevertheless, while night-shift operations create depression, additional dilemmas developed from night-shift operations are night-shift anxiety. In other words, night-shift anxiety accumulates through continued night-shift or graveyard operations. For instance, businesses seek maximum profits through efficient 24/7 operation. Unfortunately, while businesses operate in a 24/7 environment, individuals who operate a night or graveyard shift develop anxiety symptoms resulting from sleep depression. Thus, although companies seek maximum profits, maximum profits are compromised by out-of-sync and anxious employees. As stated by Wild (2004), "Sleep deprivation results in increased irritability, anxiety, depression and decreased creativity, all of which can be caused by a combination of factors" (p. 12). In essence non-productive daytime sleep creates irritability and anxiety within family or workplace organizations. As further stated by Tamagawa (2007), "Tolerance of shift work was associated with anxiety, repressive emotional style and mood" (p. 260). Consequently, night or graveyard shift creates an anxious society resulting from aversive working conditions.

However, while night-shift anxiety is prevalent in the workplace, opportunities can be developed towards mitigating anxious symptoms. In other words, opportunities should be developed within a workplace organization, which decreases graveyard employee anxiety. Furthermore, establishing employee human concerns rather than mere talk therapy can be a start in a right direction. As stated by Milano, "Double the number of allowable absences for night workers -- it can help reduce the number of accidents by as much as 50%" (p. 1). Hence, graveyard employee considerations are necessary when employees are employed during unusual working conditions. Unfortunately, as employees report unusual graveyard conditions, employees become reprimanded leading towards further anxiety, depressive, and family-disordered conditions. Therefore, graveyard employees become expendable workplace commodities.

Nonetheless, while depression and anxiety symptoms continue from graveyard operations, night-shift social conflicts additionally continue contributing towards an existing depressed graveyard workforce. In essence being employed on a night or graveyard shift can produce an array of calamities. For instance, operating in a continuous environment produces company advantages and disadvantages. While company advantages use efficient capitol utilization, company disadvantages produces additional stress and social conflicts that are attributable towards a non-standard working setting. In other words, working a night or graveyard shift creates isolation, alienation, and family conflicts resulting from an out-of-sync irritable and anxious workforce. Nonetheless, while companies assume irregular individual behavior is a result of individual characteristics, irregular individual behavior such as irritability or social conflicts is the result of a company's creativity. As stated by Jekielek, PhD (2003), "Overall, non-standard work schedules are associated with higher levels of conflict and lower levels of positive interaction" (p. 1). In essence non-standard work schedules create social calamities, which are contributable towards company's continuous operations and non-standard work environments. As further stated by Bohle and Tilley (1998), "Night shift rated most negatively on circadian/sleep disturbance and work/non-work conflict effects" (p. 61).

On the other hand, while a graveyard shift produces social calamities, company opportunities can be developed towards mitigating social calamities. In other words, opportunities can be developed, which recognize the third-shift or graveyard worker rather than ignoring the forgotten graveyard worker. Furthermore, providing on-site social counseling with activities can alleviate social family conflicts. As stated by Solomon (1993), "HR professionals must be aware of whether the shift schedule is or is not working for the employees. Shift workers cannot be managed as afterthoughts" (p. 36). In essence human resources have an opportunity towards managing graveyard shift workers rather than ignoring graveyard shift workers or mistreating individuals as human afterthoughts. As further stated by Solomon (1993), "Surprisingly, HR managers approach these employees as if they had the same work environment as their daytime counterparts, although this clearly isn't the case" (p. 36). Therefore, challenges lie ahead for human resource professionals, which can initiate programs that will mitigate family social conflicts brought on by company environments. Surprisingly though, as graveyard employees communicate human resources concerns, human resources on the other hand, ignore graveyard employee concerns as troublesome irritable employees.

Nonetheless, as depression, anxiety, and social conflicts continue from an overburdened graveyard worker, other dilemmas continue resulting from graveyard operation. For instance, operating a graveyard or third shift becomes a challenge within oneself. In essence an individual is attempting to work while the body seeks rest. Unfortunately, while a graveyard shift has unique rewards through greater compensation, social dilemmas such as divorce through increased social conflicts can additionally occur. Thus, while compensation rewards through shift challenges serve as short-term gratifications, higher divorce rates resulting from graveyard social conflicts create long-term challenges. In sessence, company graveyard operations resulting from non-standard working conditions create increased divorce rates resulting from increased social conflicts. As stated by Rasmussen (1990), "Klein said other studies of the night shift effect on marriages have indicated that divorce rates are 25 percent higher for night shift workers than for day workers" (p. 1.M). As further stated by Stuart (1998), "In the US, the divorce rate is 60 per cent higher among shift-working families than among day-workers in regular jobs" (p. 2). As additionally stated by Pfadenhauer (2006), "The divorce rate for night-shift workers is as much as six times higher than the rest of the population" (p. 1). In essence, while companies promote family values, companies additionally promote higher divorce rates through graveyard operations. Hence, graveyard or night-shift employment is a detriment towards promoting family values.

Nevertheless, while graveyard divorce rates are increasing, opportunities can be developed, which will mitigate graveyard divorce rates. In other words, companies are encouraged towards promoting family balanced values rather than harming family balanced values. Thus, whereas workers seek relief from social conflicts, opportunities become available that decreases divorce rates resulting from graveyard social conflicts. In essence human resources must become aware of various social conflicts and divorce, which are created by graveyard shift operations. As stated by Monk (1989), "Age has been found to be a determinant of the ability to copy with shift work" (p. 26). As additionally stated by Harrar (2004), "And if you have kids, your divorce risk is three to six times higher than normal" (p. 42). Consequently, human resources have opportunities that mitigate social conflict outcomes through employee recognition rather than employee commodities or afterthoughts.

On the other hand, as depression, anxiety, social conflicts, and divorces continue from graveyard operation, graveyard fatigue additionally continues from an inadequate sleep deprived workforce. For example, individuals work unconventional hours required by society's excessive demands. Unfortunately, while individuals become employed during night or graveyard schedules, individuals encounter body challenges resulting from unconventional schedules. In essence appropriate or night-time sleep is compromised by a company's aggressive schedules. In addition as adequate sleep becomes short-changed, prolonged short-changed sleep develops into individual fatigue. Unfortunately, as individual fatigue events occur, employees become faulted for fatigue company's errors. As stated by Curran (2006), "...say people who work nights are constantly battling their own natural tendencies to sleep or wake. The longer subjects went without sleep, the crankier they got, complaining of fatigue, back pain, joint pain and upset stomachs" (p. E.3). As further stated by Dembe (2009), "In addition, studies show that fatigue-related errors made by employees working in these kind of demanding schedules can have serious and adverse repercussions for public safety" (p. 195). As additionally stated by Kunert, King, and Kolkhorst (2007), "Fatigue is a critical issue for nurses that may lead to medical errors, degradation in performance, decreased mental acuity, and social problems" (p. 31). In essence fatigue created from graveyard operations can manifest into errors and reduced individual performance. However, as employees become irritable from fatigued related events, employees additionally become reprimanded from irritable events. Hence, employees can become scapegoats from company's misguided events.

However, while fatigue related events from unusual working conditions create individual challenges, company opportunities can be developed, which will diminish employee fatigued events. In essence while employee fatigue becomes part of an employee's dilemma, opportunities such as rest stations, awareness, or adequate company sleep periods are encouraged towards minimizing employee fatigue rather than promoting employee harassments, which contribute towards further fatigue events. As stated by Czeisler and Dinges (1986), "The problem is further compounded by the fact that few employers encourage workers to reveal trouble with staying awake on the job" (p. C.5). As further stated by Baxter, Ph.D. (2000), "A simple solution that is well received in European countries, but generally frowned upon in our culture, is strategic napping" (p. D.5). In essence while simple company solutions or opportunities exist, employees become ever challenged with managing human resources or fatigue related events. Furthermore, as employees attempt towards mitigating fatigue events through strategic napping, employees unfortunately, become reprimanded or terminated for strategic napping.

Nevertheless, as depression, anxiety, social conflicts, divorce, and fatigue continue resulting from night shift or graveyard operation, sleeplessness additionally continues resulting from continued non-standard working conditions. In essence night-shift or graveyard employees encounter significant human challenges. For instance, night-shift employees attempt daytime sleeping, while a majority workforce operates during daytime hours. Unfortunately, while attempts towards daytime sleep may appear successful, a build-up of an individuals sleep bank leading towards sleeplessness may yield an otherwise dilemma. As stated by Pepper and Kay (2004), "Night-shift workers may be more alert, but what happens when they then try to sleep during the day? They might not sleep at all, and sleeplessness has its perils" (p. 56). In essence while night-shift or graveyard workers appear alert, sleeplessness is lingering or creeping in the background. As further stated by Donohue, PhD. (2002), "Night shifts upset everyone's sleep patterns. The body clock is in conflict. Normally, the body clock is in synch with daylight and darkness, making the body alert when it is light and making it sleepy when it is dark" (p. F.5). In essence an individual's body is in a state of survival resulting from non-standard employment conditions.

On the other hand, while sleeplessness continues from an out-of-sync workforce, opportunities can exist, which minimizes sleeplessness conditions. In other words, since companies create non-standard working conditions, then companies through human resources should develop increased programs, which minimize a sleeplessness workforce. As stated by Donohue, PhD. (2002), "Perhaps all you need to rest soundly is treatment for them" (p. F.5). Unfortunately, a demanding society sacrifices rest for individual perils. As further stated by Sproul (1993), "…the Sleep Disorders Center at Pomona Valley Hospital Medical Center is researching the possibility that catnaps may actually be good for business" (p. B.3). Hence, while catnaps are essentially good for business through decreased sleeplessness and litigation disputes, catnaps can additionally be damaging towards employees through supervisory or human resource harassments or extinctions.

Nonetheless, as depression, anxiety, social conflicts, divorce, fatigue, and sleeplessness continue resulting from night shift or graveyard operation, night-shift disguises additionally continues resulting from company aversive practices. For instance, companies operate in a continuous environment achieving maximum productive efficiency. In addition companies have a diverse and aged workforce, who contributes towards company efficiency. However, as individuals uncover questionable or areas of concern, companies can use a graveyard shift to rid off undesirable employees. In essence an undesirable graveyard shift can create company disguises or loopholes towards aged voluntary withdrawals. In other words, since graveyard or night-shift operation presents significant human challenges, companies desire voluntary employee withdrawals created by such human challenges. Similarly, as ethnic populations become undesirables, aged or ethical workforce become victims of graveyard challenges. As stated by Kertscher (2002), "A high-ranking member of the Milwaukee County Sheriff's

Department has filed an age discrimination complaint, alleging that Sheriff David Clarke is trying to force him to quit by threatening him and making him work nights and weekends" (p. 2B). As further stated by Hodges (1990), "The suit says the captains suffered age discrimination when Police Chief Tony Bouza transferred them in 1988 and '89 from positions as precinct and investigative commanders to inspection division jobs that required them to work night shifts" (p. 3.B). As additionally stated by Rayman (1997), "…a 10-year veteran assigned to the 111th Precinct in Bayside, alleges that he was passed over for promotion, subjected to repeated inspections, punitively placed on a night shift, denied time off…" (p. A7). In essence while companies use shift work towards company efficiency, companies additionally use shift work or graveyard duties towards creating punitive voluntary withdrawals or aged removal disguises. In other words, as companies maximize profits through shift-work utilization, companies additionally use night-shift or graveyard as leverage for disguised discriminatory withdrawals or punitive damages.

However, while night-shift or graveyard positions can create company disguises, opportunities can exist, which recognize employee individuality. In other words, opportunities can exist, which transform problems into opportunities rather than transforming problems into disguised retaliatory methods. As stated by Ference (2001), "Empowering employees to do a good job

96

is made easier when employees respect their co-workers, have opportunities to continuously learn, are fairly evaluated by supervisors, and have fun" (p. 12). In essence respect towards employees can be better served and is a start than using disguised retaliatory graveyard methods.

Nevertheless, as depression, anxiety, social conflicts, divorce, fatigue, sleeplessness, and retaliatory graveyard disguises continue resulting from night shift or graveyard operation, night-shift accidents additionally continues resulting from company continuous operations. In other words, graveyard shift operations create higher accidents resulting from various individual fatigued operations. As stated by Mills (2000):

> The highest number of errors and accidents on the road is between 3am and 5am - our body's most naturally sleepy time - and disruption of the body clock has also been implicated as one of the root causes of the Chernobyl and Challenger disasters (p. 8).

Furthermore, as stated by Rajaratnam and Arendt (2001), "Industrial accidents associated with night work are common, perhaps the most famous being Chernobyl, Three Mile Island, and Bhopal" (p. 999). In essence being employed on a graveyard or night-shift can result in greater accidents caused by an individual's biological clock being out-of-sync with society's network. Yet, while graveyard conditions are known, employees become targets for company's created accidents. As additionally stated by Fortson, Ph.D. (2005), "The injury hazard is

97

substantially higher at night than during regular daytime work hours" (p. 1). In essence graveyard operation produces a greater number of accident rates resulting from an out-of-sync biological system. Furthermore, while employees desire minimal accidental operations, employees become targets towards graveyard accidental operations.

However, as companies seek efficiency towards continuous operations, companies have opportunities, which will minimize graveyard accidents resulting from graveyard operations. As stated by Kerin (2004), "Managers of extended hours operations can implement numerous interventions to address the increased risk of ergonomics injuries for the 24 million Americans who regularly work nights, rotating shifts, irregular and on-call schedules" (p. 1). In essence companies should seek toward improvements, which reduce human extended hours or graveyard related accidents. On the other hand, while companies seek out greater profits through continuous operations, companies compromise employee accidents through graveyard operations.

On the other hand, as depression, anxiety, social conflicts, divorce, fatigue, sleeplessness, retaliatory graveyard disguises, and accidents continue resulting from night shift or graveyard operation, night-shift diseases additionally continues resulting from company continuous night-time operations. As stated by Blachowicz and Letizia (2006), "Shift workers can experience loss or change in appetite, constipation, dyspepsia, heartburn, abdominal pain, and an exacerbation of ulcer and bowel disease" (p. 274). As further stated by Marino, Ph.D. (2006), "One such exposure may be night shift work, which has been associated with menstrual disruption and increased risk of two other estrogen-mediated diseases, breast cancer and adverse coronary events" (p. 1). In essence while night shift has short-term compensation benefits, an array of diseases created from night-shift operation exceed any short-term rewards from night-shift operation. As additionally stated by McDonald (2004), "It disrupts the body's circadian rhythms, that is, its daily cycle, causing tiredness, mental stress, cardio-vascular diseases, gastro- intestinal disorders, menstrual disorders, reproductive system dysfunction and increased accidents" (p. 11). Thus, as night-shift employees seek assistance through human resources, night-shift employees become treated as sub-humans while addressing individual concerns. In essence while companies provide night-shift or graveyard employee compensation benefits, companies additionally reward employees through graveyard diseases brought on by a disruptive human biological clock system.

However, while night-shift diseases occur resulting from night-shift or graveyard operation, opportunities become available that reduces employee night-shift diseases. In other words, while a graveyard shift appears as a necessary business operation, opportunities can exist that reduces individual diseases resulting from such graveyard operation. As stated by Josling (1999), "Yet the scientific research that has been done points clearly to the imperative need for minimal night work, the abolition of rotating shifts, adequate time for meal breaks and lengthy rest periods between shifts" (p. 1). In essence while short-term graveyard compensation appears as a reward for unusual working conditions, eradicating graveyard diseases should be a preferred choice of operation.

Nevertheless, as depression, anxiety, social conflicts, divorce, fatigue, sleeplessness, retaliatory graveyard disguises, accidents, and diseases continue resulting from night shift or graveyard operation, night-shift cancers additionally continues resulting from company continuous operations. In essence while night-shift or graveyard employees seek protection from various graveyard calamities, night-shift or graveyard employees encounter cancers brought on by graveyard operation. As stated by Schernhammer, Laden, Speizer, Willett, et al (2001):

> Women who work on rotating night shifts with at least three nights per month, in addition to days and evenings in that month, appear to have a moderately increased risk of breast cancer after extended periods of working rotating night shifts (p. 1563).

Thus, as companies strive towards achieving maximum efficiency through continuous operation, companies strive towards developing cancers for night-shift or graveyard employees. As further stated by Schernhammer and Schulmeister (2004), "Cancer is the second leading cause of death in industrialised countries like the United States, where a significant proportion of workers engage in shift work, making a hypothesised relation between light exposure at night and cancer risk relevant" (p. 941). However, as employees search for human resources communications through company awareness, employees become undesired targets towards silencing graveyard communications. In other words, communicating company concerns is rewarded through punitive and silenced graveyard operation. As additionally stated by the International Agency for Research on Cancer (IARC) (2007), "Epidemiological studies have found that long-term nightworkers have a higher risk of breast cancer risk than women who do not work at night. These studies have involved mainly nurses and flight attendants" (p. 1).

Nevertheless, as cancer graveyard challenges continue, companies have opportunities, which will minimize cancer graveyard challenges. In essence, opportunities become prevalent in a workplace, which can minimize graveyard cancers. In addition companies desire healthy employees combined with a safe environment. Therefore, companies can provide a healthy work atmosphere minimizing exposures towards cancer creating environments. In other words, as employees contribute individual skills and talents towards a productive company, companies should not provide cancerous rewards for individual efforts. Unfortunately, as graveyard cancerous conditions become known, companies will simply ignore headed warnings through further undesired working conditions or disguised terminations.

Nonetheless, as depression, anxiety, social conflicts, divorce, fatigue, sleeplessness, retaliatory graveyard disguises, accidents, diseases, and cancers continue resulting from night shift or graveyard operation, night-shift legal damages additionally continues resulting from company continuous operations. In other words, although continuous company operations using maximum utilization appears profitable, legal and punitive damages resulting from accidents, diseases, and other dilemmas can eradicate any company profits resulting from continuous human operation. As stated by Randall (2003), "Studies have pinned the price tag of fatigue-related accidents and injuries to U.S. businesses at roughly $77 billion each year, including cleanup costs, fines, lawsuits, and lost productivity" (p. 38). As further stated by Hazelwood (2003), "More recently, a New Jersey jury found Conrail liable for $52.4 million in damages to the family of an employee killed in an accident caused by another employee who said he was operating on only three to four hours of sleep" (p. 1).

In essence graveyard or night-shift accidents are converted towards company punitive damages resulting from a fatigued workforce. As additionally stated by Epstein (2009), "A jury in New Brunswick has awarded a Flemington man $1 million in compensatory damages after finding his bosses in United Parcel

102

Service's North Jersey district illegally retaliated against him because he complained about possible fraud in the district" (p. 1). Furthermore, as stated by Epstein (2009), "Michael Battaglia, 51, was demoted from his position as a manager to a supervisor and assigned to the night shift after lodging his complaints in October 2005, according to the lawsuit he brought against UPS" (p. 1). Hence, while companies seek maximum profitability through continuous operations, maximum profitability's are invites towards recapturing through graveyard fatigued and diseased punitive measures.

Nonetheless, while punitive measures are prevalent from a fatigued and diseased workforce, opportunities are ever present, which can minimize such a fatigued and diseased workforce. In other words, companies have an opportunity towards realizing employees are human beings rather than human afterthoughts, who desire a reasonable and safe working environment. In essence employees desire safe working conditions, which do not produce graveyard fatigued and diseased conditions. As stated by Fitzgibbon (2006), "As Diane says, workers on the night shift will sometimes receive a premium for working nights. But there are things that money can't compensate for" (p. 1). In other words, acquiring graveyard cancers, diseases, social calamities, and other undesirable events cannot be replaced by minor company compensation. Unfortunately, as employees communicate adverse events towards higher or human resource management, adverse events will continue towards employees resulting from "GODless" companies. As stated by Norman Jr. and Zavalla (2007):

> We as a society have become so complacent that we are becoming a nation of "do nothing" until it is too late. Now we are becoming a godless society that is giving away our rights right and left because we are not speaking up for what is right and what our country was founded upon, that is a belief in God and what he stands for (p. 1).

Stakeholder Perspectives/Ethical Dilemmas

However, while graveyard employees encounter graveyard challenges, stakeholders from employees to shareholders focus towards resolving ethical graveyard dilemmas. In other words, stakeholders attempt towards minimizing graveyard working conditions while achieving company efficiency through rewards on company investments. As stated by Davies (1992), "Establishing safe and healthy working conditions not only avoids legal problems, but is also sound management" (p. 4). Unfortunately, while employees contribute towards achieving company goals, graveyard employees can become scapegoats for company dilemmas, which invite legal challenges or other punitive measures.

For instance, company employees desire adequate working conditions, which encourage health and safety in a workplace. Furthermore, employees anticipate respect, which allows employees accomplishing company goals. Regrettably, treatment of company employees as graveyard afterthoughts does not contribute towards ethical stakeholder practices. In essence graveyard employee stakeholders become ethical dilemmas towards company's business practices. In other words, graveyard employees while stakeholders become company legal challenges through acquired graveyard dilemmas.

Nonetheless, while employee graveyard stakeholders encounter challenges through promoting company goals, upper management strives towards achieving balances between company employees and shareholders. In essence upper management focuses on company goals through efficient utilization of all capital resources. In addition upper management seeks approval from shareholders through efficient company operations and meeting company's operational objective. In other words, upper management's goal achieves a company's mission through shareholder guidance and a support team of loyal company employees. As stated by Kaptein (1999), "It is the task of the company's management to find a balance between the conflicting interests employees face and to ensure that the balance is institutionalized" (p. 625). In other words, employees or stakeholders receive conflicting health and safety messages while companies promote graveyard conditions that create graveyard calamities. As further stated by Lorca and Garcia-Diaz (2004), "The long term survival of the firm requires to carry out a balance between inducements and contributions of all the stakeholders" (p. 93). In other words, every company stakeholder from employees to shareholders is required for company survival, which surprisingly is an 'Amazing Graze' principle.

Nevertheless, while upper management seeks balance between employees and shareholders through efficient operations, shareholders seek realistic and ethical returns on shareholders investments. In essence company shareholders desire adequate return on investment (ROI). In addition company shareholders seek adequate ROI through ethical business practices. Furthermore, while shareholders desire maximum profits, an ethical balance must be achieved through proper upper management business practices. As stated by Ardichvili, Mitchell, and Jondle (2009), "That is, the purpose of business is not to just make money. Rather, it is to provide a 'good balance of customer value and profit' and 'giving back to the community in which the company does business' (p. 445). In essence shareholders or stakeholders desire ethical returns combined with community presence rather than providing graveyard diseases and reoccurring punitive measures from stakeholders or other agencies. In essence company shareholders anticipate ethical business practices. Unfortunately though, as stated by Epstein, McEwen, and Spindle (1994), "The survey results indicate that many shareholders do not expect a high level of ethical behavior from corporate employees or officers" (p. 447). As further stated by Epstein, McEwen, and Spindle (1994), "However the majority would sacrifice profits for ethical behavior

106

(58%) and most would prefer at least limited disclosure about ethics in the annual report (72%)" (p. 447). Hence, while employees or shareholders desire safe and healthy working conditions, upper management or stakeholders sacrifice employees working conditions for short-term company profits. However, while short-term profits create short-term rewards, graveyard calamities resulting from social calamities or diseases generate long-term damages, which eradicate a company's short-term profits. As stated by Randall (2003), "The 24/7 economy may look profitable on paper, but not if potential profits are eaten up by lawsuits and skyrocketing insurance premiums" (p. 37). Hence, graveyard employee stakeholders are compromised for company short-term profits through unethical business practices brought on by a "GODless" society.

End-State Vision

While stakeholders, being employees, upper management, or shareholders, encounter graveyard calamities brought forth through company's business practices, individuals or leaders seek solutions towards minimizing graveyard calamities. In essence individuals or leaders gather available data and design solutions, which prevent reoccurrence from graveyard calamities. As stated by the University of Phoenix (2009) end-state-vision section of a GAP analysis section, "A true leader not only works on solving the problem, but also thinks beyond the crisis by implementing measures to prevent the problem from happening again"

(p. 5). In essence leaders seek futuristic opportunities provided by current capabilities, which decreases or eliminates graveyard calamities created by company's excessive demands.

For instance, night shift or graveyard employees encounter challenges brought on through unusual or night shift working conditions. Nonetheless, while night shift or graveyard employees encounter calamities, night shift or graveyard employees seek awareness through acceptance of graveyard calamities. As stated by the Journal of Nuclear Medicine (2007), "…the growing awareness that sleep-deprived interns working 24-hour shifts make many more serious medical errors while working in intensive care units and crash their cars more often…" (p. 44N). In essence seeking acceptance through awareness may be a first step towards recognizing graveyard calamities and becoming fully aware that graveyard calamities will occur resulting from adverse and unusual working conditions. As further stated by Horne and Revner (1999), "Time of day (circadian) effects are profound, with sleepiness being particularly evident during night shift work, and driving home afterwards. Self awareness of sleepiness is a better method for alerting the driver than automatic sleepiness detectors in the vehicle" (p. 289).

In essence while company employees seek awareness through acceptance of graveyard calamities, company management on the other hand, seeks denial of graveyard calamities. In addition awareness towards recognizing graveyard employees are not human afterthoughts might encourage human resources or others to seek alternate paths towards creating a productive workforce. Furthermore, when night shift or graveyard employees desire improvements towards adverse working conditions, human resources acknowledgement through acceptance rather than avoidance or rejection should be an approved response.

Nonetheless, while graveyard conditions require awareness, acceptance, and the first step towards acknowledgement, visionaries seek additional solutions towards conquering graveyard calamities. For example, night shift or graveyard employees encounter various challenges brought on through unusual working environments. Challenges, which are encountered in the workplace, are often discussed with other licensed professional using talk therapy. In essence using talk therapy can assist towards finding alternative solutions towards existing dilemmas. In addition using talk therapy can create awareness of calamities brought forth by graveyard conditions. However, while talk therapy provides awareness of graveyard calamities, licensed professionals have an opportunity towards intervening with company human resources creating further awareness and reassignments towards alleviating graveyard challenges. In essence licensed professionals have opportunities towards improving an individuals well being through interaction of a company's human resources and not be constrained within certain boundaries. In essence talk therapy is converted towards action therapy through human resource interaction. Thus, as continued talk therapy resulting from graveyard calamities produces additional talk therapy, then alternate methods or action therapy through company interaction is encouraged, which solves graveyard calamity events.

Similarly, as talk therapy is transformed towards action therapy, walk the talk principles are applied towards talk therapy. As stated by Maguire (1996), "The walk is how an organization turns its talk into reality" (p. 20). In other words, outcome of talk therapy is reflected upon an organization requiring action therapy, which transforms a graveyard society encountered by calamities towards a humanistic society encountered by individual growth. In essence effective talk therapy can be transformed towards action therapy using appropriate intervention communication tools.

Nonetheless, while action therapy remains a visionary challenge towards improving graveyard calamities, other visionary challenges are available towards minimizing graveyard calamities. For instance, companies are often stressed towards achieving maximum profits brought on by shareholder demands. In essence achieving maximum profits through efficient usage of company resources creates enhanced profits. Furthermore, achieving efficient company capital resources was established through 24/7 or continuous shift operations. However, while continuous shift operations can eradicate company profits through graveyard calamities, graveyard challenges can be overcome through automation, robotics, or other humanoid intervention, which achieves continuous company operation without encountering graveyard calamities. In essence a gradual shift towards humanoid graveyard operation can prevail towards continuous company operation. In other words, while the human receives his or her night rest, the humanoid, avoidance of coffee or other breaks, can adequately perform night-time humanistic operations.

As stated by the Economist (2005), "Corporate rivalry, advancing technology and a desire for publicity, together with a fascination for machines that resemble their human creators and the distant prospect of a vast new market, have conspired to create a fresh breed of robots" (p. 3). As further stated by the Economist (2005), "But now Japan's industrial giants are spending billions of yen to make such robots a reality" (p. 3). In essence while humans are enjoying respective day-time employment activities, humanoids can become a productive member of society through night-time employment activities. As further stated by Torrance (2008), "In what ways should we include future humanoid robots, and other kinds of artificial agents, in our moral universe" (p. 27)? In essence since companies seek towards overcoming economic challenges while maintaining competitive advantages, companies can therefore, increase technological inventions towards humanoid or human robot production, which will enhance a company's competitive advantage.

Nevertheless, while awareness, action therapy, and humanoids become available towards decreasing graveyard calamities, companies, on the other hand, may choose towards ignoring available methods, which reduce graveyard calamities. For instance, companies desire operating efficiency through continuous or 24/7 business operations by maximizing existing capital resources. However, while continuous plant operations create maximum efficiency, companies are becoming aware or recognizing graveyard calamities through various media and regulatory resources. In addition creative government stimulators or incentives were developed enabling companies towards achieving graveyard robotics or humanoid operations. Unfortunately, while government stimulators become available towards minimizing graveyard calamities, companies appear unmotivated towards protecting graveyard workers and continue unchanged operation brought forth from government regulations.

Hence, legal intervention brought forth by companies neglecting graveyard calamities and or advanced business operations through automation are required towards minimizing graveyard calamities and providing adequate protection of a society's workforce. As stated by Lunman (1990), "Crown prosecutor Bob Sigurdson asked for stiff penalties for both companies because they failed to take action after employees noticed trench walls slipping weeks before Vrabec's death. He accused the firms of ignoring regulations to save time and money" (p. B.7). As further stated by Wilson (2005), "By moving to 24-hour living, and reducing or ignoring the dark bit, we are effectively throwing away the advantages of millions of years of evolution" (p. 8). In essence legal intervention through gradual punitive damages is required for ignoring graveyard calamities, which will restore improved health, safety, and social organizations to desired levels.

Gap Analysis

While end-state visions provide futuristic opportunities towards humanistic improvements, graveyard calamities developed from the industrialized revolution through economic and company expansions yields incentives for further humanistic improvements. In other words, should conditions of graveyard calamities provide alternative solutions, incentives, or encouragement towards improving workplace conditions, which will create or enhance an existing workforce? In essence understanding industrialized effects towards graveyard contributions will lead towards improvements in an existing workforce.

The industrial revolution brought many inventions, which led towards economic and company expansions. For instance ease of automotive production through creative ingenuity such as mass production created similar manufacturing ideas, which contributed towards economic enhancements. In addition developing light sources using Thomas Edison's invention allowed use of company's expansion through continuous or 24/7 operation. In essence industrialized inventions, such as light at night, created company expansions of human and fixed capital resources. As stated by Forward, Beach, Gray, and Quick (1991), "The industrial revolution from manufacturing to mentofacturing involves developing organizations that emphasize learning, human development, risk-taking, and technology transfer" (p. 32). As further stated by Tucker (2005), "It was the factory system, however, that had the most dramatic impact on the production process and helped to change the economic and social direction of the new nation" (p. 21). In other words, the industrial revolution brought forth an abundance of opportunities developed from various manufacturing processes, which provided economic and company expansions resulting from develpmental activities.

However, while the industrial revolution created many opportunities and allowed for continuous company operations, graveyard calamities resulting from 24/7 or continuous operation is an additional outcome created from unusual working conditions resulting from continuous operations. A graveyard calamity is a condition created as a result of unusual working conditions, which produces depression, anxiety, social conflicts, divorce, fatigue, sleeplessness, retaliatory graveyard disguises, accidents, diseases, cancer, or other unknown symptoms brought onward through a company's unusual work schedules. In other words, although the industrial revolution created various and extended opportunities resulting from light-at-night developments, unfortunate bi-products such as graveyard calamities created many industrial tragedies. As stated by Burgess, MD, MPH (2006), "The Presidential Commission on the space shuttle *Challenger* accident cited the contribution of human error and poor judgment related to sleep loss and shift work during the early morning hours" (p. 1). As further stated by Burgess, MD, MPH (2006), "The incidents involving the Bhopal Union Carbide tragedy and the *Exxon Valdez*, as well as the *Estonia* ferry incident, all occurred in the early morning hours" (p. 1). In essence while an industrial revolution created many opportunities, industrial tragedies from light-at-night become unfortunate challenges towards visionary improvements. Furthermore, while individuals encounter keep-awake strategies during unusual working conditions, individuals additionally encounter reprimands resulting from unusual or night shift fatigued errors.

On the other hand, companies seek maximum efficiency using fixed and human capital resources benefited by light-at-night capabilities. In addition companies have automated processes, which provided an additional competitive advantage. In essence combining light-at-night with automated processes allows companies to achieve a strategic advantage without the perils of graveyard calamities. As stated by Zwiebach (2004), "In all, the report concluded, nearly one hundred night shift cleaning workers in the state meatpacking industry suffered amputations and crushings of body parts in the period (1999-2003) reviewed by the investigative team" (p. 5). Hence, while light-at-night company operations using human capital appears beneficial, usage of automated or humanoid light-at-night operations appears as an alternative advantage. Furthermore, since company challenges seek economic improvements, while maintaining strategic advantages, company challenges using humanoids, automatic processes, robotics, or other non-human capital resources can be efficiently used during unusual work environments. In other words, robots, humanoids, or other automated processes are not confronted by labor laws requiring breaks, meal times, smoke times, or other labor law requirements.

Conclusion

Companies or individuals are ever faced with challenges brought forth through various business challenges. In addition companies overcame business challenges using light-at-night advantages. In essence light-at-night capabilities enabled businesses maximum usage of fixed and human capital resources. Hence, using light-at-night principles allowed companies to achieve maximum daily output.

However, while companies achieve rewards from light-at-night activities, companies additionally develop perils from light-at-night activities. In other words, while companies achieve short-term rewards from night-shift or graveyard conditions, individuals gain long-term perils from graveyard calamities. On the other hand, while stakeholders being employees, upper management, or shareholders desire ethical working conditions, company profits may often supercede or take precedence to working conditions. Nonetheless, while end-state-visions create opportunities or alternate solutions towards mitigating graveyard calamities, graveyard calamities will continue unless change towards graveyard calamities will be administered. Furthermore, while society is directed towards "GODless" conditions, significant change must be overcome, which recognizes graveyard calamities. As stated by Hickey, (2005), "The vast majority of good, upright citizens fear that if they speak up for what is right and moral, they will be slandered" (p. B.11).

Recommendation

Problems are often encountered describing various symptoms. However, while problems are encountered, opportunities towards viable solutions are developed using end-state-vision principles. In other words, solutions are encountered prevented repeated events, which provide future opportunities. Unfortunately, graveyard calamities are problems requiring modifications. In essence, when graveyard calamities affect millions, which has the potential for further calamities then change or recommendations becomes a necessity. Nonetheless, end-state-visions, through gap analysis research, provide informative solutions towards existing dilemmas. However, while analyzing end-state-visionary objectives, awareness towards acceptance may be the first step towards recognizing graveyard calamities. Therefore, when graveyard calamities are accepted, then further visionary concepts can be established towards achieving a greater humanistic workforce.

References

Abrams, L. (1987). Night shifts are for the birds. *Off Our Backs,* 17(4), 8. Retrieved March 2, 2009, from ProQuest database.

Allday, E. (2008). Keeping the 'grave' out of 'graveyard shift.' *San Francisco Chronicle,* A1. Retrieved March 13, 2009, from website http://www.sfgate.com/cgi-bin/article.cgi?f=/c/a/2008/03/24/MNGPVK33E.DTL&type=printable.

Ahuja, A. (2004). Turn out the night. *The Times,* 14. Retrieved February 26, 2009, from ProQuest database.

Anonymous (2007). Extended Hours Tied to Errors for Medical Trainees. *The Journal of Nuclear Medicine,* 48(2), 44N(2). Retrieved April 18, 2009, from ProQuest database.

Ardichvili, A., Mitchell, J. A., & Jondle, D. (2009). Characteristics of Ethical Business Cultures. *Journal of Business Ethics,* 85(4), 445(7). Retrieved April 8, 2009, from ProQuest database.

Baxter, M. L. Ph.D. (2000). Lack of sleep may damage your health. *Standard,* D.5. Retrieved March 19, 2009, from ProQuest database.

Berger, A. M. & Hobbs, B. B. (2006). Impact of Shift Work on the Health and Safety of Nurses and Patients. *Clinical Journal of Oncology Nursing,* 10(4), 465(7). Retrieved March 1, 2009, from ProQuest database.

Blachowicz, E. & Letizia, M. (2006). The Challenges of Shift Work. *Medsurg Nursing,* 15(5), 274(7). Retrieved March 2, 2009, from ProQuest database.

Bohle, P. & Tilley, A. J. (1998). Early experience of shiftwork: Influences on attitudes. *Journal of Occupational and Organizational Psychology,* 71(1), 61(19). Retrieved February 25, 2009, from ProQuest database.

Burgess, P. A., MD, MPH (2006). Optimal Shift Duration and Sequence: Recommended Approach for Short-Term Emergency Response Activations for Public Health and Emergency Management. *American Public Health Association,* 1. Retrieved May 1, 2009, from website http://www.pubmedcentral.nih.gov/articlerender.fcgi?artid=1854972.

Czeisler, C. & Dinges, D. (1986). Drowsy workers may be the cause of major disasters. *Toronto Star,* C.5. Retrieved March 19, 2009, from ProQuest database.

Curran, P. (2006). Night workers battle fatigue. *The Vancouver Sun,* E.3. Retrieved February 26, 2009, from ProQuest database.

Davies, J. E. (1992). Enhancing Life at the Interface. *Library Management,* 13(3), 4(6). Retrieved April 7, 2009, from ProQuest database.

Dembe, A. E. (2009). Ethical Issues Relating to the Health Effects of Long Working Hours. *Journal of Business Ethics,* 84, 195(14). Retrieved February 26, 2009, from ProQuest databse.

Donohue, P., PhD. (2002). Chronic sleeplessness exacts its toll. *Edmonton Journal,* F.5. Retrieved February 27, 2009, from ProQuest database.

Economist (2005). Humanoids on the march. *The Economist,* 374(8417), 3. Retrieved April 21, 2009, from ProQuest database.

Epstein, E. (2009). Flemington man was demoted, put on night shift after fraud complaints. *The Star-Ledger,* 1. Retrieved March 27, 2009, from ProQuest database.

Epstein, M. J., McEwen, R. A., & Spindle, R. M. (1994). Shareholder preferences concerning corporate ethical performance. *Journal of Business Ethics,* 13(6), 447(7). Retrieved April 9, 2009, from ProQuest database.

Ference, G. (2001). Improving organizational performance: Using survey-driven databases. *Cornell Hotel and Restaurant Administration Quarterly,* 42(2), 12(16). Retrieved March 23, 2009, from ProQuest database.

Fitzgibbon, M. (2006). The Risks of Working the Night Shift. *Canadian Labor and Employment Law,* 1. Retrieved March 28, 2009, from website http://labourlawblog.typepad.com/managementupdates/2006/09/the_ris ks_of_wo.html.

Fong-Torres, B. (1988). KRQR's New Team; KKCY Becomes KHIT. *San Francisco Chronicle,* 58. Retrieved February 28, 2009, from ProQuest database.

Fortson, K. N., Ph. D. (2005). Economic analysis of workplace injuries. *Princeton University,* (100). Retrieved March 23, 2009, from ProQuest database.

Forward, G. E., Beach, D. E., Gray, D. A., & Quck, J. C. (1991). Mentofacturing: A Vision for American Industrial Excellence. *The Executive,* 5(3), 32(13). Retrieved April 29, 2009, from ProQuest database.

Josling, L. (1999). Shift work and ill-health. *World Socialist Web Site,* 1. Retrieved March 24, 2009, from website

http://www.wsws.org/articles/1999/sep1999/shift-s06.shtml.

Han, W. J. (2007). Nonstandard Work Schedules and Work-Family Issues. *Columbia University – School of Social Work,* 1. Retrieved May 5, 2009, from website

http://wfnetwork.bc.edu/encyclopedia_entry.php?id=5854&area=All.

Harrer, S. (2004). Night shift's hidden danger. *Prevention,* 56(5), 42. Retrieved April 26, 2009, from EBSCOhost database.

Hazelwood, K. (2003). Scary Truths about the Graveyard Shift. *BusinessWeek,* 1. Retrieved March 2, 2009, from website

http://www.businessweek.com/bwdaily/dnflash/jul2003/nf20030711_447 4_db035.htm.

Hickey, R. (2005). We are becoming a godless society. *Sudbury Star,* B.11. Retrieved May 7, 2009 from ProQuest database.

Hodges, J. (1990). Minneapolis police captains' suit charging age discrimination settled. *Star Tribune,* 3.B. Retrieved February 28, 2009, from ProQuest database.

Horne, J. & Revner, L. (1999). Vehicle accidents related to sleep: A review. *Occupational and Environmental Medicine,* 56(5), 289(6). Retrieved April 18, 2009, from ProQuest database.

Horrocks, N. & Pounder, R. (2006). Working the night shift: preparation, survival, and recovery. *Royal College of Physicians of London,* (24). Retrieved March 3, 2009, from website http://209.85.173.132/search?q=cache:T0IUKCcCBhgJ:www.rcplondon.ac.uk/pubs/books/nightshift/nightshiftbooklet.pdf+night+shift+legal+consequences&hl=en&ct=clnk&cd=24&gl=us&client=firefox-a

Hossain, J. L., PhD (2004). Sleep, fatigue and sleepiness in shift-workers and sleep-disordered individuals. *University of Toronto (Canada),* 242. Retrieved February 26, 2009, from ProQuest database.

International Agency for Research on Cancer (2007). Shiftwork that involves circadian disruption is "probably carcinogenic to humans." *International Agency for Research on Cancer,* 1. Retrieved March 25, 2009, from website http://www.iarc.fr/en/Media-Centre/IARC-Press-

Releases/Communiques-recents/IARC-Monographs-Programme-finds-

cancer-hazards-associated-with-shiftwork-painting-and-firefighting

Jackson Jr., H. (2005). Night workers need a good day's sleep. *Knight Ridder Tribune Business News,* 1. Retrieved February 23, 2009, from ProQuest database.

Jekielek, S. M., PhD. (2003). Non-standard work hours and the relationship quality of dual-earner parents. *The Ohio State University,* 142. Retrieved February 25, 2009, from ProQuest database.

Kaptein, M. (1999). Integrity management. *European Management Journal,* 17(6), 625. Retrieved April 7, 2009, from ProQuest database.

Kerin, K. (2004). New Erogonomics Research Shows Many Extended Hours Workers May Be at Unecessary Risk Of Injury. *PR Newswire,* 1. Retrieved March 23, 2009, from ProQuest database.

Kertscher, T. (2002). Sheriff's official alleges age bias. *Milwaukee Journal Sentinel,* 2.B. Retrieved February 28, 2009, from ProQuest database.

Kunert, K., King, M. L., & Kolkhorst, F. W. (2007). Fatigue and Sleep Quality in Nurses. *Journal of Psychosocial Nursing & Mental Health Services,* 45(8), 31(7). Retrieved March 18, 2009, from ProQuest database.

Kyodo News Int. (2002). 1 in 3 night-shift employees complain of health problems. *Japan Weekly Monitor,* 1. Retrieved February 27, 2009, from PowerSearch database.

Lasalandra, M. (2001). Studies link night shifts to breast cancer risk. *Boston Herald,* 020. Retrieved March 2, 2009, from ProQuest database.

Lorca, P. & Garcia-Diez, J. (2004). The Relationship between Firm Survival and the Achievement of Balance among its Stakeholders: An Analysis. *International Journal of Management,* 21(1), 93. Retrieved April 8, 2009, from ProQuest database.

Lunman, K. (1990). Calgary firms fined by judge in slide death. *Calgary Herald,* B.7. Retrieved April 22, 2009, from ProQuest database.

Maguire, B. (1996). How to walk the talk. *The Journal for Quality and Participation,* 19(3), 20(6). Retrieved April 20, 2009, from ProQuest database.

Marino, J. L., Ph.D. (2006). Occupation, shift work, and T3111C hCLOCK polymorphism and risk of endometriosis. *University of Washington,* (107). Retrieved March 24, 2009, from ProQuest database.

McDonald, L. (2004). HEALTH: A working nightmare; Late-shift workers die younger than day staff. Lucy McDonald reveals how to survive the dark side of employment. *The Independent,* 11. Retrieved March 2, 2009, from ProQuest database.

Milano, C. NIGHT WORKERS FACE ARRAY OF DIFFICULTIES. Retrieved March 14, 2009, from website

http://www.nasw.org/users/milanocarol/nightshift.html.

Mills, M. (2000). Health: Doing nights: Britain is now open 24 hours a day – but experts warn that we are not meant to be awake at night. Merope Mills on the dangers of working from dusk to dawn. *The Guardian,* 8. Retrieved March 1, 2009, from ProQuest database.

Monk, T. H. (1989). Shift Work And Safety. *Professional Safety,* 34(4), 26(5). Retrieved March 18, 2009, from ProQuest database.

Norman Jr., J. C. & Zavalla (2007). Letter: Yes, it does matter. *Lufkin Daily News,* 1. Retrieved March 28, 2009, from ProQuest database.

Parry, R. (2008). Noisy vehicles disturb society. *Times – Colonist,* A7. Retrieved February 25, 2009, from ProQuest database.

Pepper, T. & Kay, S. (2004). Night Shift; In a 24-hour society, when are people supposed to get a good night's rest? Scientists have made great strides in figuring out how the body regulates the sleep cycle, and they're coming up with ways of circumventing it. *Newsweek,* 56. Retrieved February 27, 2009, from ProQuest database.

Perry-Jenkins, M., Goldberg, A. E., Pierce, C. P., & Sayer, A. G. (2007). Shift Work, Role Overload, and the Transition to Parenthood. *Journal of Marriage and Family,* 69(1), 123(16). Retrieved February 23, 2009, from ProQuest database.

Pfadenhauer, D. (2006). Perils of the Graveyard Shift. *Strategic HR Lawyer*, 1. Retrieved March 18, 2009, from website http://www.strategichrlawyer.com/weblog/2006/09/perils_of_the_g.html .

Randall, A. L. (2003). Risk Never Sleeps. *Contingencies*, 37(5). Retrieved March 3, 2009, from Circadian Technologies.

Rajaratnam, S. MW. & Arendt, J. (2001). Health in a 24-h society. *The Lancet*, 358(9286), 999(7). Retrieved March 1, 2009, from ProQuest database.

Rasmussen, J. (1990). Company Trains Employees to Cope Night Shift Lifestyle 'Affects Everything.' *Omaha World – Herald*, 1.M. Retrieved February 26, 2009, from ProQuest database.

Rayman, G. (1997). Cop Sues NYPD / Latino officer says his criticism led to harassment. *Newsday*, A.07. Retrieved March 21, 2009, from ProQuest database.

Ruggiero, J., PhD. (2002). Correlates of fatigue in critical care nurses. *Rutgers The State University of New Jersey*, 133. Retrieved February 23, 2009, from ProQuest database.

Schernhammer, E. S. & Schulmeister, K. (2004). Melatonin and cancer risk: does light at night compromise physiologic cancer protection by lowering serum melatonin levels? *The British Journal of Cancer,* 90(5), 941. Retrieved March 2, 2009, from ProQuest database.

Schernhammer, E. S., Laden, F., Speizer, F. E., Willett, W. C., & et al (2001). Rotating Night Shifts and Risk of Breast Cancer in Women Participating in the Nurses' Health Study. *Journal of the National Cancer Institute,* 93(20), 1563. Retrieved March 2, 2009, from ProQuest database.

Solomon, C. M. (1993). HR is solving shift-work problems. *Personnel Journal,* 72(8), 36(9). Retrieved March 15, 2009, from ProQuest database.

Sproul, S. (1993). Catnaps Might Boost Job Performance. *San Francisco Chronicle,* B.3. Retrieved March 19, 2009, from ProQuest database.

Stuart, L. (1998). When 9-to-5 seemed a nice number. *The Guardian,* 2. Retrieved February 26, 2009, from ProQuest database.

Tamagawa, R. (2007). Anxiety; Research from University of Auckland provide new insights into anxiety. *Mental Health Weekly Digest,* p. 260. Retrieved February 25, 2009, from ProQuest database.

Torrance, S. (2008). Ethics and consciousness in artificial agents. *AI & Society,* 22(4), 495(27). Retrieved April 21, 2009, from ProQuest database.

Tucker, B. M. (2005). Liberty is Exploitation: The Force of Tradition in Early Manufacturing. *Magazine of History,* 19(3), 21(4). Retrieved April 30, 2009, from ProQuest database.

University of Phoenix (2009). MBA GAP Analysis Template. Retrieved April 17, 2009, from the University of Phoenix writing templates.

Violanti, J. M., PhD. (2008). University at Buffalo; Researchers investigate impact of stress on police officers' physical and mental health. *Psychology & Psychiatry Journal,* 14. Retrieved February 25, 2009, from ProQuest database.

Wild, A. (2004). Tiredness … or just plain lazy?; The lure of sleep can prove irresistible but research suggests this could be caused by biological programming. *The Herald,* p. 12. Retrieved February 24, 2009, from ProQuest database.

Wilson, H. (2005). G2: Health: The power of darkness: Artificial light illuminates our lives, allowing us to work or play through the night. But, as Hugh Wilson discovers, we toy with our body clocks at severe risk to our wellbeing. *The Guardian,* 8. Retrieved April 22, 2009, from ProQuest database.

Zwiebach, P. (2004). An American Tragedy: The Decline of U.S. Unionism and its Human Rights Implications. *Human Rights & Human Welfare,* 5, 101(11). Retrieved May 1, 2009, from website http://209.85.173.132/search?q=cache:WJ0qipqS3FsJ:www.du.edu/korbel/hrhw/volumes/2005/zwiebach-

2005.pdf+night+shift+industrial+tragedies&cd=12&hl=en&ct=clnk&gl=

us

Table 1

Issue and Opportunity Identification

Issue	Opportunity	Reference to Specific Course Concept (Include citation)	Concept
Society is operating in a 24/7 environment, which requires workers operating various shifts resulting in working against an individuals biological clock. Furthermore, operating against an individual's biological clock causes an individual being out-of-sync with society and their social well being. In essence being out of sync with social society's network invites alienation and depression.	Opportunities can be developed through awareness and company quality improvements, which will minimize night-shift depression resulting from an alienated workforce.	"People who work nights (upset) that circadian rhythm (the 24- hour body clock)," said Geralyn Frandsen, associate professor of nursing at Maryville University. "You suffer from depression because you don't see the sun ... you have personal conflicts within your family; it can cause loneliness, depression, substance abuse when people use (chemicals such as medication or alcohol) to get to bed ... " (Jackson, 2005,	Night-shift depression

		p. 1).	
		"These findings suggest that depression and poor sleep quality are more prevalent in night shift nurses than day shift nurses. Depression and sleep quality are significant correlates of chronic fatigue" (Ruggiero, 2002, p. 1)	
		"Multilevel modeling analyses revealed that working evening or night shifts, as opposed to day shifts, was related to higher levels of depressive symptoms. Results suggest that for new parents, working nonday shifts may be a risk factor for depressive symptoms and	

		relationship conflict" (Perry-Jenkins, Goldberg, Pierce, & Sayer, 2007, p. 123).	
Businesses seek maximum profits through efficient 24/7 operation. Unfortunately, while businesses operate in a 24/7 environment, individuals who operate a night shift develop anxiety symptoms resulting from sleep depression. Thus, although companies seek maximum profits, maximum profits are compromised by out-of-sync and anxious employees.	Opportunities can be developed, which decreases employee anxiety. Furthermore, establishing employee human concerns rather than mere talk is a start in a right direction.	"Sleep deprivation results in increased irritability, anxiety, depression and decreased creativity, all of which can be caused by a combination of factors" (Wild, 2004, p. 12). "This excessive noise also causes anxiety for shift workers, who are disturbed in the daytime when they try to catch up on their sleep. Nurses, doctors, police, public transit drivers and a host of others are required to work at night, usually for our benefit" (Parry, 2008, p. A.7).	Night-shift anxiety

		"Tolerance of shift work was associated with anxiety, repressive emotional style and mood" (Tamagawa, 2007, p. 260).	
Operating in a 24/7 environment produces company advantages and disadvantages. While company advantages use efficient equipment utilization, company disadvantages produces additional stress and conflicts that is attributable towards non-standard working conditions. In other words, working a third shift creates isolation, alienation, and family conflicts resulting from an out-of-sync individual. Nonetheless, while companies assume irregular individual behavior is a result of individual characteristics, irregular individual behavior such as irritability is the result of a company's creativity.	Opportunities can be developed, which recognize the third-shift or graveyard worker. In addition providing on-site social counseling with activities can alleviate social conflicts.	"On the other hand, higher suicide ideation reported by males on the midnight shift may be accounted for in part by a stronger need to be part of the social cohesiveness associated with peers in the police organization. Working alone at night without the support of immediate backup can be stressful" (Violanti, PhD, 2008, p. 14). "Overall, non-standard work	Night-shift social conflicts

		schedules are associated with higher levels of conflict and lower levels of positive interaction" (Jekielek, PhD, 2003, p. 1) "Night shift rated most negatively on circadian/sleep disturbance and work/non-work conflict effects" (Bohle & Tilley, 1998, p. 61).	
Operating a graveyard or third shift becomes a challenge within oneself. In essence an individual is attempting to work while the body seeks rest. Unfortunately, while the graveyard shift has unique rewards through greater compensation, social dilemmas such as divorce thru greater conflicts can additionally occur. Thus, while rewards serve as short-term gratifications, higher divorce rates from social conflicts create long-term dilemmas.	While workers seek relief from social conflicts, opportunities become available that decreases divorce rates resulting from social conflicts.	"Klein said other studies of the night shift effect on marriages have indicated that divorce rates are 25 percent higher for night shift workers than for day workers" (Rasmussen, 1990, p. 1.M). "'The health of night-shift workers is clearly impaired, whether we are talking about	Night-shift divorce

| | | cardiovascular disease, depression, sleep abnormalities or psychosocial problems such as divorce,' says Foster, Professor of Molecular Neuroscience at Imperial College in London" (Ahuja, 2004, p. 14).

"In the US, the divorce rate is 60 per cent higher among shift-working families than among day-workers in regular jobs" (Stuart, 1998, p. 2). | |
| Individuals work unconventional hours required by society's demands. Unfortunately, while individuals work night or graveyard schedules, individuals encounter body challenges. In essence proper sleep is compromised by company schedules. In addition as proper sleep becomes short-changed, | While employee fatigue becomes part of an employees dilemma, opportunities such as rest stations, awareness, or adequate sleep | "...say people who work nights are constantly battling their own natural tendencies to sleep or wake. The longer subjects went without sleep, the crankier they got, complaining | Night-shift fatigue |

prolonged short-changed sleep develops into individual fatigue. Unfortunately, as individual fatigue events occur, employees become faulted for fatigue company's errors.	periods are encouraged towards minimizing fatigueness.	of fatigue, back pain, joint pain and upset stomachs" (Curran, 2006, p. E.3) "Excessive fatigue is a very common complaint in shift-workers and sleep-disordered individuals. However, fatigue is often equated with excessive sleepiness and thus rarely studied as an independent symptom of disordered sleep" (Hossain, PhD, 2004, 242 pgs.) "Considerable research evidence has accumulated indicating that there is an increased likelihood for illness and injury among employees working in long-	

		hour schedules and schedules involving unconventional shift work (e.g., night and evening shifts). In addition, studies show that fatigue-related errors made by employees working in these kind of demanding schedules can have serious and adverse repercussions for public safety" (Dembe, 2009, p. 195).	
Night-shift or graveyard employees encounter significant challenges. For instance, night-shift employees attempt daytime sleeping, while a majority workforce operates during daytime hours. Unfortunately, while attempts towards daytime sleep may appear successful, a build-up of an individuals sleep bank leading towards sleeplessness may yield otherwise.	Since day time sleeping leading towards sleeplessness is a challenge, opportunities can be developed towards minimizing sleeplessness.	"Night-shift workers may be more alert, but what happens when they then try to sleep during the day? They might not sleep at all, and sleeplessness has its perils" (Pepper & Kay, 2004, p. 56).

"Night shifts upset everyone's | Night-shift sleeplessness |

		sleep patterns. The body clock is in conflict. Normally, the body clock is in synch with daylight and darkness, making the body alert when it is light and making it sleepy when it is dark" (Donohue, PhD, 2002, F.5)	
		"One out of three private-sector employees who work night shifts complains of bad health, some of them suffering from gastrointestinal disorders, illnesses associated with high-blood pressure, or sleeplessness, according to a government survey" (Kyodo News, 2002, p. 1)	
Individuals discover areas for improvement in a workplace.	Opportunities can exist,	"When KNBR transferred him	Night-shift disguises

In addition companies operate in a 24/7 environment seeking towards maximizing productivity efficiency. However, as individuals uncover areas of concerns, companies can use a graveyard shift to rid off undesirable workers. In essence an undesirable graveyard shift can create disguises towards aged voluntary withdrawals.	which transform problems into opportunities rather than transforming problems into retaliatory methods.	from daytime duties to the all-night shift in 1985, he sued the station and owner NBC, claiming discrimination and retaliation for previous complaints he'd filed against the company. Now, Kim's out of a job" (Fong-Torres, 1988, p. 58). A high-ranking member of the Milwaukee County Sheriff's Department has filed an age discrimination complaint, alleging that Sheriff David Clarke is trying to force him to quit by threatening him and making him work nights and weekends (Kertscher, 2002, p. 2B). "The suit says	

		the captains suffered age discrimination when Police Chief Tony Bouza transferred them in 1988 and '89 from positions as precinct and investigative commanders to inspection division jobs that required them to work night shifts" (Hodges, 1990, p. 3.B).	
Companies operate in a 24/7 environment to improve productivity. Unfortunately, while operating in a 24/7 environment, accidents occur resulting from out-of-normal operating condition.	Companies have an opportunity towards decreasing accidents resulting from 24/7 operation.	"The highest number of errors and accidents on the road is between 3am and 5am - our body's most naturally sleepy time - and disruption of the body clock has also been implicated as one of the root causes of the Chernobyl and Challenger disasters" (Mills, 2000, p. 8).	Night-shift accidents

		"For example, sleepiness surpasses alcohol and drugs as the greatest identifiable and preventable cause of accidents in all modes of transport. Industrial accidents associated with night work are common, perhaps the most famous being Chernobyl, Three Mile Island, and Bhopal" (Rajaratnam & Arendt, 2001, p. 999). "Shift work disrupts the synchronous relationship between the body's internal clock and the environment. The disruption often results in problems such as sleep disturbances,	

		increased accidents and injuries, and social isolation" (Berger & Hobbs, 2006, p. 465).	
Operating on a graveyard shift is a challenge onto oneself. In addition operating a graveyard shift becomes increasingly challenging as individuals age. Nonetheless, while individuals operate a graveyard shift, individual diseases increase resulting from operating outside of a body's parameters. In essence graveyard employment introduces various diseases.	While a graveyard shift appears as a necessary business operation, opportunities can exist that reduces individual diseases resulting from graveyard operation.	"Night owls, beware! If you are one of the every sixth woman is this country who works a night shift, your work may be hazardous to your health" (Abrams, 1987, p. 8). "The older the worker, the less tolerant they are to withstanding the adverse effects of shift work... It disrupts the body's circadian rhythms, that is, its daily cycle, causing tiredness, mental stress, cardio-vascular diseases, gastro- intestinal disorders, menstrual	Night-shift diseases

| | | disorders, reproductive system dysfunction and increased accidents" McDonald, 2004, p. 11).

"Shift workers can experience loss or change in appetite, constipation, dyspepsia, heartburn, abdominal pain, and an exacerbation of ulcer and bowel disease" (Blachowicz & Letizia, 2006, p. 274). | |
|---|---|---|---|
| While operating a graveyard shift offers short-term rewards, operating a graveyard shift in addition offers long-term illnesses. In essence operating a graveyard shift exposes an individual to cancer. | Opportunities are prevalent in a workplace. In addition companies desire healthy employees. Therefore, companies can ensure a healthy environment minimizing exposures | "Women who work on rotating night shifts with at least three nights per month, in addition to days and evenings in that month, appear to have a moderately increased risk of breast cancer after extended periods of | Night-shift cancers |

	towards cancer environments.	working rotating night shifts" (Schernhammer, Laden, Speizer, Willett, et al, 2001, p. 1563). "Researchers suggest the bright lights used at night cut the body's supply of melatonin, a protector against breast cancer, and increase the level of estrogen in the body. Estrogen can fuel the growth of breast cancer" (Lasalandra, 2001, p. 20). "Cancer is the second leading cause of death in industrialised countries like the United States, where a significant proportion of workers engage in shift work, making a hypothesised relation between light exposure at	

		night and cancer risk relevant" (Schernhammer & Schulmeister, 2004, p. 941).	
While companies operate in a 24/7 environment, legal consequences resulting from night-shift accidents create damages effects towards company profits. In essence legal damages arm profits. Furthermore, when individual safety is compromised for company profits, then legal damages will occur.	Companies have an opportunity to realize that company employees are human beings. In essence company employees desire safe working conditions.	"More recently, a New Jersey jury found Conrail liable for $52.4 million in damages to the family of an employee killed in an accident caused by another employee who said he was operating on only three to four hours of sleep" (Hazelwood, 2003, p. 1). "Studies have pinned the price tag of fatigue-related accidents and injuries to U.S. businesses at roughly $77 billion each year, including cleanup costs, fines, lawsuits, and lost productivity"	Night-shift legal consequences

		(Randall, 2003, p. 38). "Working at night, regardless of the shift pattern, can have consequences for both patient and personal safety, as it increases the risk of making poor decisions or even mistakes. It is therefore important to learn how to prepare for night shifts and to manage your sleep, so that you minimise risk to yourself and to your patients" (Horrocks & Pounder, 2006, p. 4).	

Table 2

Stakeholder Perspectives

Stakeholder Perspectives	
Stakeholder Groups	**The Interests, Rights, and Values of Each Group**
Company shareholders	Company shareholders desire adequate return on investment (ROI). In addition company shareholders seek adequate ROI through ethical business practices. In essence while shareholders desire maximum profits, an ethical balance must be achieved through proper upper management business practices.
Company management team	Upper management strives towards achieving balance between company employees and shareholders. In essence upper management focuses on company goals through efficient utilization of resources. In addition upper management seeks approval from shareholders through efficient company operations and meeting company's operational objective.
Company employees	Company employees desire adequate working conditions, which encourages health and safety in a workplace. In addition employees anticipate respect, which allows employees accomplishing company goals. Unfortunately though, treating employees as human switches or afterthoughts discourages employee value.

Table 3

End State Goals

End-State Goals
Night shift or graveyard employees encounter challenges brought on through unusual working conditions. Nonetheless, while night shift or graveyard employees encounter calamities, night shift or graveyard employees seek awareness through acceptance of graveyard calamities. In essence seeking acceptance through awareness may be a first step towards recognizing graveyard calamities and becoming fully aware that graveyard calamities will occur resulting from adverse and unusual working conditions. Furthermore, awareness towards recognizing graveyard employees are not human after thoughts might encourage human resources or others to seek alternate paths towards creating a productive workforce.
Night shift or graveyard employees encounter various challenges brought on through unusual working environments. Challenges, which are encountered in the workplace, are often discussed with other licensed professional using talk therapy. In essence using talk therapy can assist towards finding alternative solutions. In addition using talk therapy can create awareness of calamities brought forth by graveyard conditions. However, while talk therapy provides awareness of graveyard calamities, licensed professionals have an opportunity towards intervening with company human resources creating further awareness and reassignments towards alleviating graveyard challenges. In essence licensed professionals have opportunities towards improving an individuals well being through interaction of a company's human resources. In essence talk therapy is converted towards action therapy through human resource interaction.
Companies are often stressed towards achieving maximum profits brought on by shareholder demands. In essence achieving maximum profits through efficient usage of company resources creates enhanced profits. Furthermore, achieving efficient company resources was established through 24/7 or continuous shift operations. However, while continuous shift operations can eradicate company profits through graveyard challenges, graveyard challenges can be overcome through automation, robotics, or other humanoid intervention, which achieves continuous company operation without encountering graveyard calamities. In essence a gradual shift towards humanoid graveyard operation can prevail towards continuous company operation.
Companies desire operating efficiency through continuous or 24/7 business operations. However, while continuous plant operations create maximum efficiency, companies are becoming aware or recognizing graveyard calamities. Furthermore,

creative company stimulators were developed enabling companies towards achieving graveyard robotics operations. Unfortunately, companies appear unmotivated towards protecting the graveyard worker and continue unchanged operation. Hence, legal intervention of graveyard calamity brought forth by companies neglecting graveyard calamities and or advanced business operations.